THE MONUMENTAL HISTORY

OF THE

EARLY BRITISH CHURCH.

THE

MONUMENTAL HISTORY

OF THE

EARLY BRITISH CHURCH.

BY

J. ROMILLY ALLEN,

F.S.A. (SCOT.)

AUTHOR OF THE VOLUME OF RHIND LECTURES ENTITLED "EARLY CHRISTIAN
SYMBOLISM IN GREAT BRITAIN AND IRELAND."

Facsimile reprint by
LLANERCH PUBLISHERS
Felinfach.
ISBN 0 86143 048 5

LONDON:
SOCIETY FOR PROMOTING CHRISTIAN KNOWLEDGE,
NORTHUMBERLAND AVENUE, CHARING CROSS, W.C.;
43, QUEEN VICTORIA STREET, E.C.; 97, WESTBOURNE GROVE, W.
BRIGHTON: 135, NORTH STREET.
NEW YORK: E. & J. B. YOUNG & CO.
1889.

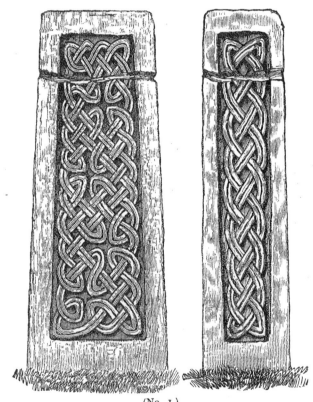

(No. 1.)

Panels of regular Plaitwork and broken Plaitwork, on
Cross-shaft, at Llantwit Major.
(From the "Archæologia Cambrensis.)

Scale $\frac{1}{12}$ real size.   *Frontispiece.*

PREFACE.

So much has been already written upon the historical side of the question as to how and when Christianity was first introduced into this country, that it is very doubtful whether the further study of ancient documents will ever be the means of throwing more light upon the subject. The archæological side of the question, however, seems to have been so far overlooked that it is not possible to mention the name of any author who has attempted to tell the story of the Early Church in Great Britain as revealed by the structures, monuments, and portable relics which still remain. For instance, if it is necessary to prove that a Saxon ecclesiastical building formerly existed in a particular locality, Doomsday Book, or the Cartularium Saxonicum, is quoted, but the examination of the spot might reveal the fact that there was a sculptured stone there with Hiberno-Saxon ornament upon it, which would constitute evidence of equal value. In other words, a complete archæological survey, showing the geographical distribution of such monuments, would

enormously extend our knowledge of the number of
early Christian sites, yet no real attempt has been
made to draw up an exhaustive catalogue of these
most interesting remains, nor have their proper
guardians taken care, in all instances, to preserve
them from the effects of disintegration by the weather.

The size of the present volume prevents the
archæological history of the Early Church in Great
Britain being dealt with except in quite a superficial
way. It is intended merely to give a general idea of
the nature of the materials that are available for
writing a more complete treatise. The chief object
the author has had in view has been to collect together, in a handy form, a considerable amount of
information that has been hitherto beyond the reach
of the general reader, either because it was contained
in rare and expensive books, or only to be found
buried in the back volumes of the proceedings of
learned societies.

An endeavour has been made to arrive at as reliable
conclusions as possible, by examining the greatest
number of specimens of each class of remains, but
the critic who is inclined to differ with the author is
reminded that no scientific deduction can be more
than a working hypothesis, liable to be controverted
at any moment by a new discovery. Thus, since this

small book has gone through the press, Mr. R. Blair announces the finding of a Christian Roman tombstone at one of the stations on the Roman Wall,[1] quite upsetting the previously accepted opinion that nothing of the kind existed in England.

The Author has to thank Mr. R. Blair, Mr. A. G. Langdon, and the Committee of the Cambrian Archæological Association for some of the illustrations. He also wishes to testify to the courteous assistance afforded him by Mr. A. W. Franks and Mr. C. H. Read of the British Museum.

In conclusion, the critic is entreated not to forget the notice said to have been posted up in a place of musical entertainment in America to this effect: " Please do not shoot the performer, as he is doing his best."

[1] *Athenæum*, Nov. 9, 1889, p. 642.

SYLLABUS OF CONTENTS.

———❖———

CHAPTER I.

THE ARCHÆOLOGY OF THE ROMANO-BRITISH CHURCH (BEFORE A.D. 400).

STRUCTURES OF THE ROMANO-BRITISH CHURCH.

CHAPTER II.

ARCHÆOLOGY OF THE EARLY CELTIC CHURCH
(A.D. 400–600).

CHAPTER III.

ARCHÆOLOGY OF THE LATER CELTIC CHURCH
(A.D. 600 TO 1006).

Irish architecture of the later Celtic Church, a local variety of Romanesque, resulting from Continental influence acting on the native Pagan methods of building—Characteristics of the Romanesque style in Lombardy—The substitution of the arch for the lintel for spanning openings—The arch used constructionally by the Romans, but disguised by sham entablatures—The arch first made of importance both in the

SEPULCHRAL AND OTHER MONUMENTS OF THE
LATER CELTIC CHURCH.

.. ——

CHAPTER V.

THE ARCHÆOLOGY OF THE SAXON CHURCH
(A.D. 600 TO 1066).

SEPULCHRAL AND OTHER MONUMENTS.

PORTABLE OBJECTS OF THE SAXON CHURCH.

LIST OF ILLUSTRATIONS.

————◆◇◆————

MONUMENTAL HISTORY

OF THE

EARLY BRITISH CHURCH.

———◆◇◆———

CHAPTER I.

THE ARCHÆOLOGY OF THE ROMANO-BRITISH CHURCH
(BEFORE A.D. 400).

IT may be well to inquire at the outset what
branches of science (or exact knowledge deduced
from ascertained facts) enable us to form our
ideas of the kind of life led by the human race
in bygone ages, in order to show what sources of
information are available for completing the picture
of the state of the early British Church as given in
history. In the first place, there is the science of
anthropology, or the study of the various races of
man, their habits, manners, customs, and ceremonies.
It deals with man in the present rather than in the
past, but throws light on the successive stages of the
advance of civilisation by calling attention to survivals in remote districts of races, customs, and ceremonies, which have become extinct elsewhere for
many centuries. Thus the Eskimos still exist as the
last remnant of the pre-Aryan population that for-

merly inhabited the greater part of Northern Europe during the glacial period; and the aborigines of Australia, who have not yet got beyond the use of stone as a material for the manufacture of cutting tools, remain as living representatives of the neolithic man.[1] With regard, then, to early Christianity, it may be possible that we shall find the history of the Celtic Church elucidated by studying the religious ceremonies practised at the present day by the Nestorian or Coptic priests.

The next science to be considered is that of philology, which treats of the growth and development of language. It will be of help in explaining such place-names or words as are connected with the establishment of Christianity in this country, and in fixing the approximate age of ecclesiastical documents.

Palæography, or the science of writing, shows how the forms of letters have varied at different periods, thus enabling the dates of MSS. or inscribed monuments to be arrived at with tolerable accuracy.

The science of folklore includes all researches connected with traditions, myths, and legends.

Lastly, the science of archæology is concerned with any structure, monument, object, or document produced by man in past ages.

Summing up, then, it appears that direct information as to what has taken place in former times can only be derived either from tradition (that is, knowledge of events handed down by word of mouth from one generation to another) or from history (that is, events

---

[1] See Prof. Boyd Dawkins's "Early Man in Britain."

described in a MS., a printed book, on an inscribed monument or object) ; but indirectly a great deal more may be learned of past civilisations by the anthropologist, who studies man himself,—his habits, manners, customs, ceremonies, occupations, and amusements ; by the philologist, who traces the development of his language ; the palæographer, who classifies the various forms of his written letters ; by the student of folklore, who investigates the evolution of his myths and legends ; and by the archæologist, who endeavours to work out a consistent theory as to his state of culture existing in different areas at different periods by means of the works of human production found there.

The necessity for archæological research arises from the imperfections or entire absence of historical records during particular periods and in special geographical areas. In the pre-historic or non-historic period, therefore, we must rely entirely on the indirect methods of obtaining information already referred to, and even when history exists, archæology is of the utmost possible value in confirming its truth or exposing its errors.

One of the chief objects in writing the present volume is to show how far the history of the early Christian Church in Great Britain can be elucidated by a careful examination of the vestiges it has left behind it, in the shape of ecclesiastical structures, sepulchral monuments, and portable relics.

In order to avoid all possibility of misconception, it may be well here to point out the relative functions of the historian and the archæologist.

The materials with which the former has to deal are original MSS., printed books, and inscriptions on structures, monuments, or objects recording the occurrence of particular events connected with human affairs, such as the births, deaths, and doings of illustrious personages ; or events connected with the universe, such as eclipses, appearance of comets, earthquakes, floods, and other phenomena of nature. All public and private documents in the nature of treaties, charters, or deeds establishing the ownership of property, and pedigrees, also fall within the province of the historian. By using his critical faculty he is able to eliminate doubtful, contradictory, or impossible statements, his object being to arrive at the true facts, and from them to build up a consistent theory of the progress of events in each country, and to show in what way these events have affected the material welfare and development of civilisation of the various branches of the human race.

The materials upon which the archæologist, on the other hand, bases his conclusions are the works of man within any given geographical area. Dr. Joseph Anderson ably explains, in his " Scotland in Early Christian Times," that the archæological method in dealing with specimens consists (1) in arranging them in groups possessing certain characteristics in common ; (2) in determining the special types of which these groups are composed ; (3) in determining the geographical range of each special type ; (4) in determining its relations to other types within or beyond its own special area ; and (5) in determining the sequence of the types existing within the geographical area which is the field of study. He goes on to say that "The general outcome of the whole dealing of the archæologist with his materials is the construction of a logical history of the human occupation of the area which he subjects to investigation,—that is a history which is not chronological, and can never become so, unless where it touches the domain of record, and by this contact acquires an accidental feature which is foreign to its character." This passage has been quoted at length because it enunciates a most important principle, and one which is continually ignored by writers on the subject. Even history itself is not necessarily chronological (*i.e.*, including the element of time), and there is no archæological process for determining the date of a specimen. Thus if the time of the occurrence of an event recorded in history is not given, there is no conceivable way of finding out exactly when it took place, unless it is connected with some other event of known date, or with an individual of known pedigree. History without dates is in fact like an engineer's drawing without a scale by which to measure the different parts of the design. The only way of fixing the date of an archæological specimen is either by direct or indirect reference to chronological history. Its age cannot be ascertained exactly unless there is a written, printed, or inscribed record relating to it, and cannot be ascertained even approximately except by comparison with other specimens of known date belonging to the same type.

The materials for archæological investigation may be classified under the heads of " Structures," "Sepul-

chral, or other Monuments," and "Portable Objects."
The inscriptions occurring on these structures, monuments, and objects are also included amongst the
materials, for although the events recorded in such
inscriptions fall within the domain of history, their
geographical distribution, &c., are fit subjects for
antiquarian research. The various specimens are
arranged in groups possessing common characteristics
by studying their material, forms, dimensions, state
of preservation, method of construction, and ornamental features. The purpose for which a structure
or object is intended can generally be determined
from its form by comparison with ones of a similar
kind in use at the present day.

The state of preservation of a specimen as regards
the effects of age is one guide for deciding the
genuineness of its antiquity, as in the case of bronzes,
which acquire that beautiful green coating known
technically as "patina" in the course of time, or of old
glass which becomes iridescent, or of a flint implement whose surface loses its original dull black
colour after long exposure.

The method of construction and the ornamental
features afford a guide for arranging the specimens
in a series according to the amount of skill exhibited
in the former and the quality of the art of the
latter.

Material is a clue to age in particular localities
where the human race has passed through successive
stages of development—(1) when man was ignorant of
the use of metals, and used stone for the manufacture
of his cutting implements ; (2) when he had discovered

bronze; and (3) when bronze was superseded by iron for most purposes.

The style of the decoration of a specimen is generally the best means of deciding whether it belongs to the geographical area in which it is found, or whether it has been imported from elsewhere; but peculiar forms, methods of construction, and material are also, in many cases, evidence of foreign origin.

In addition to the information thus to be obtained from an exhaustive examination of the specimen itself, a great deal more may be learned by knowing the exact position in which it was found, and what other specimens were associated with it. For instance, in making excavations on the site of a city such as London, each layer of *débris* which is dug through represents the accumulated rubbish of successive generations. At the top we find, perhaps, coins of the Georges, in the next stratum a mediæval ring, then a Saxon grave slab, then a piece of Roman pottery, and at the bottom of all, resting on the original surface of the ground, is disclosed the stone implement of the prehistoric man. Hence position may settle the relative age of a specimen, and association may also do the same thing, as when a specimen is found with a coin or with a flint, bronze, or iron implement.

Having now briefly sketched out the methods by which the archæologist arrives at his conclusions, we shall proceed to apply them to the elucidation of the rise and progress of the Christian Church in Great Britain as shown by its structures, monuments, and relics.

Structures.

The problem now before us is to determine how far archæology supports history in the statement that a Christian Church existed in Great Britain previous to the departure of the Romans in A.D. 410, by proving that buildings of undoubted Roman origin were used as Christian places of worship or possess any features which are distinctively Christian. In discussing this question we must endeavour to look at the matter dispassionately, and to avoid as much as possible that party spirit, which is so fatal to forming an impartial opinion on any subject whatever. Let us not on the one hand blindly follow the lead of the late Sir J. H. Parker, of Oxford, who declined to believe in the existence of Saxon ecclesiastical structures older than the eleventh century; but on the other hand let us be very sure of our facts before we accept the conclusions of those enthusiasts who are anxious to push back the date of the origin of British Christianity to its most extreme limit. In archæology, as in many other sciences, there appear to be alternate waves of opinion, at one time tending towards over-credulity and at another towards becoming over-sceptical. We have lately passed through a stage of excessive scepticism with regard to the age of pre-Norman buildings, and it may be necessary to go a little in the opposite direction in order to adjust the balance. It must, however, always be borne in mind that our object is to arrive at truth, and that by making out a thing to be older than it really is we do not necessarily increase its value, for often reducing its age may bring it within a period in which its associations become infinitely more interesting.

The historical statements with regard to the existence of Christianity in Great Britain during the time of the Roman occupation [1] are so meagre and unsatisfactory, that, unless they are confirmed by archæological research, it is impossible to attach much importance to them. St. Chrysostom, writing A.D. 367, refers in general terms to the British Islands as possessing churches, and Gildas, writing A.D. 564, says that churches existed in this country before the departure of the Romans, but neither of these authors mentions any particular place having a church nor its dedication. The first reference to a definite place, namely, Canterbury, where a church (*i.e.*, an actual structure) was believed to have existed during the Romano-British period, is in Bede's " Ecclesiastical History " (bk. i. ch. 26), written A.D. 731. The archæological method of dealing with the structural remains belonging to any particular geographical area is to arrange the individual specimens in groups possessing certain common characteristics. The structures belonging specially to the area in question, and not resembling those in any other part of the world, will form the principal group, and others possessing features common to structures found elsewhere may be formed into derived groups.[2] It is obvious that the

---

[1] For summary of information on this subject, consult Haddan and Stubbs, " Councils and Ecclesiastical Documents."

[2] Dr. J. Anderson's " Scotland in Early Christian Times " (1st series), p. 77.

date of the introduction of a derived group of structures into any area cannot be earlier than the origin of the type in the foreign country whence it came. Applying this principle to the churches of the Romano-British period, we find that they form a derived group of structures, the plan of which was introduced into this country from Rome. It is impossible, therefore, that any church in Great Britain can be older than those which were first erected in Rome. Christian worship was confined almost exclusively to the recesses of the Catacombs at Rome during the first three centuries, and it was not until after the edict of Milan, A.D. 312, that basilicas were allowed to be built above ground. As it would take some time for church-building to spread from Rome to Gaul, and then from Gaul to Britain, it seems very improbable that any Christian buildings can have existed in this country before the middle of the fourth century. There are thus about fifty years left of the period of the Roman occupation during which churches may possibly have been erected in Britain, and we will now inquire whether the remains of such churches are still in existence. The determination of whether a building is of Roman origin or not must be the work of a specialist. The chief characteristic of Roman masonry is that it is built of small square stones with courses of brick at regular intervals, examples of which may be seen at York, Lincoln, and elsewhere. The average size of the bricks is 15 in. by 10 in. and 2½ in. thick. Roman mortar may be distinguished from other kinds of cement by the pounded brick and oyster-shells with which it was mixed. Besides the general appearance of the masonry, other indications of the Roman origin of a building are obtained from its shape, from the character of the objects dug up on its site, and from the fact that certain towns, such as those whose names end in "chester," are known historically to have been founded by the Romans. For the purposes of our investigation, however, it will be necessary to prove that the structures we intend to examine are not only of Roman origin, but that they were also used as churches. The ecclesiastical origin of a building is often difficult to determine, as the plans of the first churches were copied from those of the secular basilicas or halls of justice at Rome. The chief points to be observed are whether the building is rightly orientated by being placed with its longer axis due east and west;[1] whether it is associated with Christian burials; whether the altar remains *in situ ;* whether Christian symbols occur in the decoration ; and, lastly, whether any inscriptions are found throwing light on its use. No building in Britain as yet discovered on a Roman site, or otherwise ascertained to be Roman, and not used as a church at present, has been proved by any of the above tests to have been constructed for ecclesiastical purposes. The only question is whether any of the churches still in use can be shown to be wholly, or partly, of Roman construction, and whether there is any proba-

---

[1] This is, however, not always a satisfactory test, as the churches in Rome itself are not always properly orientated (see E. P. Loftus Brock in "Trans. S. Paul's Eccl. Soc.," vol. ii. p. 214, and T. Barnard in "Assoc. Arch. Soc. Reports," vol. i. p. 175).

bility of their having been intended, in the first instance, to do duty as places of Christian worship. There are a great many churches in England, in the building of which Roman materials have been freely used, but evidently either in Saxon times, or later. Examples of the use of Roman bricks in the building of churches exist at Brixworth, Northamptonshire ; at Dover Castle, St. Paul's Cray, Southfleet, Chalk, Burham, Lower Halstone, Leeds, and Lyminge, in Kent. The ancient city of Verulam was used as a quarry, whence an ample supply of bricks was obtained for building St. Alban's Abbey and the Church of St. Michael at St. Albans. Roman altars have been utilised at Daglingworth in Gloucestershire, to make a window ; at Staunton, Herefordshire, and Haydon Bridge, Northumberland, for fonts. The fonts at Kenchester, Herefordshire ; and Wroxeter, Shropshire, are formed out of Roman columns, and Roman sculptured stones are built into the walls of Ilkley Church, Yorkshire ; of Escomb Church, co. Durham ; of the crypt at Hexham, and in many other instances. The fact of the materials being thus re-used suggests the probability that the present churches are of post-Roman date,[1] although some are Saxon, and it is possible that a few of the buildings which were pulled down and rebuilt may have been earlier churches on the same site, though no proof can be given that this was the case.

In addition to the above mentioned, there are

[1] Roman materials were, however, sometimes utilised over again even in Roman times, as in the case of the walls of Chester. See J. P. Earwaker's " Roman Remains at Chester."

some very remarkable instances in Kent, at Reculver, Canterbury, and Lyminge, of not merely bricks and stones from Roman buildings being utilised, but of actual Roman walls forming part of the present churches.

We will now proceed to examine these at some length. The village of Reculver is situated on the north coast of Kent, near the mouth of the Thames, eight miles north-east of Canterbury, and about three miles from Herne Bay. The Roman station, remains of which still exist at this place, was called Regulbium, and at the time it was built commanded the northern entrance to the river Wantsum, then flowing between the Isle of Thanet and the mainland of Kent, in the same way that Rutupiæ, or Richborough, commanded the southern entrance. In the time of Leland (A.D. 1530 to 1537), the Castrum stood a quarter of a mile from the sea, but the encroachments have been so great since, that only the south wall and part of the east and west walls now remain standing. A plan, dated 1685, engraved in Mr. C. Roach Smith's "Richborough, Reculver, and Lympne," shows the Castrum complete with the north wall close to the edge of the cliff; but when Mr. Boys, of Sandwich, made his survey in 1780 for the "Bibliotheca Topographica," the north wall had fallen into the sea. The Castrum was originally a rectangle enclosing an area of nearly eight acres.

The wall is 8 ft. high, and from 8 ft. to 10 ft. wide, built of alternate layers of flint and septaria, but without the courses of brick which are characteristic of Roman masonry generally. The surface of the inside of the Castrum is level with the top of the wall.

The ruined Church of Reculver is situated in the middle of the Castrum, and all that now remains of the building are the two western towers and part of the walls of the nave and chancel. The towers escaped destruction not from any feeling of reverence, but because they were useful as a landmark for ships entering the Thames, and were purchased in 1809 by the Trinity Board to preserve them for that purpose. The wall surrounding the churchyard was entire in 1805, but owing to high tides and violent storms the cliff crumbled away so rapidly after this that in 1809 the sea had advanced within five yards of the north angle of the tower. The rapid encroachment of the sea just about this time appears to have been due principally to the greed for gain on the part of the inhabitants, who took up the stone-work which protected the foot of the cliff and sold it to the Margate Pier Company for the foundation of their new pier. The church was wantonly pulled down by the vicar and his parishioners in 1809, since which time it has remained a ruin. The plan consisted of a nave, 66 ft. by 24 ft., with aisles at each side, 8 ft. 9 in. wide ; a chancel, 44 ft. by 24 ft. ; and two western towers giving a frontage of 65 ft. outside.

The greater part of the work is Norman with early English additions, but there are certain features still existing which show that the core of the church, round which the rest was built, is of Roman date. Before the destruction in 1809, the chancel was separated from the nave by two pillars supporting three arches of unequal span, the centre one being the largest. The columns, which still exist, are of oölite, 17 ft. high; 2 ft. in diameter at the bottom, and tapering to 1 ft. 6 in. at the top ; having their capitals and bases ornamented with cable mouldings. The arches were turned in Roman brick, and the walls at each side were built of square stones with three bands of brick after the Roman fashion. Only the lower part of these walls now remains, but a drawing of the whole in its original state was made by Mr. Joseph Gandy, A.R.A., and is published by Mr. C. Roach Smith in his " Richborough, Reculver, and Lympne," p. 197.

The history of the re-discovery of the whereabouts of the pillars, after being missing for half a century is somewhat remarkable. The publication of Mr Gandy's drawings, just mentioned, led Mr. J. B. Sheppard, of Canterbury, to inquire into the matter, and he found that when the church at Reculver was abandoned on account of the encroachments of the sea, some of the materials were sold, and the rest used to build a new church at Hillborough, further inland. Amongst the materials sold were the two columns, which were purchased by Mr. Francis, of Canterbury, and placed in his orchard. Here they were discovered by Mr. Sheppard, who was enabled at once to identify them by means of Mr. Gandy's drawings. These precious relics of early Christianity in Great Britain are now safely preserved within the precincts of Canterbury Cathedral, in a garden on the north side.

Mr. Sheppard says of them:—"The interest attached to these columns arises from the fact that, although forming part of a fourteenth-century church, they are not Gothic ; they are too artistically proportioned and executed to be Romanesque ; and they are classical in style and outline ; so that, if the second of these propositions be indisputed, it must follow they are Roman ; and if Roman, their size and importance demand that they be considered part of some stately edifice, probably a temple or basilica of Regulbium."[1]

Mr. George Dowker has recently made investigations at Reculver, by which he has been able to trace out the complete plan of the Roman building.[2] In addition to the columns and arches of the wall separating the nave from the chancel, Mr. Dowker has found that the three square piers on each side of the nave, and the semi-circular apse beneath the chancel are built of Roman masonry. The whole of the nave, two side aisles, and chancel, as far as the end of the semi-circular apse, is paved with concrete, consisting of a basis of boulders, overlaid with mortar like that used in Roman work, and faced with red pounded tile, brought to a smooth polished surface.

Parts of the original walls of the chancel standing are seen 6 ft. in height, and 2 ft. 6 in. in width, built of very compact masonry, with layers of Roman tiles. The interior of the early church must have been at

[1] C. Roach Smith's "Collectanea Antiqua," vol. vi. p. 226, quoted from "Proc. Soc. Ant., Lond.," 1861, p. 369.
[2] "Archæologia Cantiana," vol. xii. p. 248.

least 62 ft. from east to west; the width of the nave
24 ft. and the aisles 56 ft. long by 11 ft. wide.   Mr.
Roach Smith says, in his work on "Richborough,
Reculver, and Lympne" (p. 199), previously alluded
to, that "It is altogether hopeless to ascertain what
the Roman edifice was, the remains of which formed
part of the Church of Reculver . . . .   That it was a
public structure having claims to architectural beauty,
must be inferred from the portions under consideration ;[1] probably it was either a basilica or a temple,
which, we know, served as models for the early
English churches."

With regard to the terrible piece of vandalism
committed in destroying this interesting building,
Mr. Roach Smith goes on to say :—" The church
possessed, then, especial claims for preservation.
The Roman architecture gave it a distinctive feature
of remote antiquity, of which it would be difficult to
find another example in this country.   It stood as a
monument of the downfall of paganism and the
triumph of Christianity; upwards of a thousand
years our forefathers had preserved, endowed, and
repaired it; and generation after generation had
called it theirs, and within its walls had ratified the
obligations of social life ; they had died and were
buried about it.   Tradition hallowed it as the burial
place of Ethelbert, who received and protected
Augustine.   Monuments of the ancestors of rich
and influential families, whose near relatives also lay
there interred, stood within and around its walls.
The church at the commencement of the present

[1] *I.e.*, the columns.

C

century, though it had been neglected, and was
dilapidated, might easily have been repaired; but
the gentry and clergy abandoned it to jobbers and
speculators, who seized upon the venerable pile, tore
it to pieces, and divided the spoil; and old people
who remember the circumstances, tell how the bells
fell to the share of one, the lead to another; recount
the prices at which the materials were sold, and
relate how ere long the curse of Heaven fell on all
destroyers of the church; that nothing prospered
with them, and that at last they and their families
came to misery and ruin."

These being the facts about the church at Reculver, what are the conclusions to be drawn from
them with regard to the age of its foundation? It is
probable that a Saxon church existed at Reculver
early in the seventh century, as Æthelberht, the first
Christian King of Kent, who died in A.D. 616, resided
there during the last few years of his life, and "it
long disputed with St. Augustine's Abbey the honour
of his burial place" (Dean Stanley's "Memorials of
Canterbury," p. 46). The "Saxon Chronicle" tells
us that in the year 669 Ecgbriht gave Reculf to Bass,
the mass-priest, to build a monastery thereon; and
Bede, in his "Ecclesiastical History" (bk. v. ch. 8),
says that Theodore, seventh Archbishop of Canterbury, who died in A.D. 691, was succeeded in the
episcopate by Berctwald, "who was abbot in the
monastery, which is situated near the north side of
the mouth of the river Genlada, and is called
Racuulfe."

The charter of Eadred, drawn up by Dunstan, by

which the monastery of Reculver was granted to Christ Church, Canterbury, in A.D. 949, is preserved amongst the archives of the Dean and Chapter of that place. Many Saxon and Merovingian coins found at Reculver bear witness to its early occupation in post-Roman times.

The Saxons would naturally make use of a Roman building already existing on the spot for their first church, and the only question to be decided is whether it was intended by the original builders to serve a similar purpose. There is nothing in the orientation, or in the general character of the ground-plan, to show that the Roman building was not meant to be a church in the first instance, but at the same time, no Christian symbols appear in the decorative features, nor are any Christian burials or inscriptions of the Roman period associated with it.

Until, therefore, some fresh evidence of a more conclusive nature is brought forward, the question must remain an open one.

We will next proceed to examine some other churches in Kent, for which a pre-Saxon date has been claimed.

The church at Reculver is more interesting than any other from an archæological point of view, and has, therefore, been considered first; but, historically, the early ecclesiastical buildings of Canterbury are the most important of all, as it is there that Christianity was first taught to the Saxons by St. Augustine (A.D. 597); and we have the testimony of Bede, writing A.D. 731, or 134 years after the occurrence of the events he records, that two at least of the churches at Canterbury, namely St. Martin's and the Cathedral, were restorations of structures erected by Romano-British Christians.

The passages in Bede's "Ecclesiastical History" describing the first churches in Canterbury are as follows :—

St. Martin's (bk. i. ch. 25).—"For before this (the landing of St. Augustine in the Isle of Thanet) the fame of the Christian religion had reached him, inasmuch as he had a Christian wife of the royal family of the Franks, by name Bercta (daughter of Chariberct), whom he had received from her parents on this condition, that she might have leave to keep inviolate the rite of her faith and religion with the Bishop (of Senlis), by name Luidhard, whom they had given her as an assistant of her faith."

(Bk. i. ch. 26).—"There was, moreover, near the same city (Canterbury), towards the east, a church anciently built in honour of St. Martin, *while the Romans still inhabited Britain*, in which the Queen Bercta, who, as I before said, was a Christian, was accustomed to pray."

The Cathedral (bk. i. ch. 33).—"But Augustine, when he received the episcopal see, as I before said in the royal city, recovered it, being supported by the King's assistance, a church which he learnt had been there *built by the ancient work of the Roman believers*, and consecrated it in the name of the Holy Saviour God and our Lord Jesus Christ, and there established a residence for himself and all his successors."

The Church of SS. Peter and Paul, now St. Augustine's Abbey (bk. i. ch. 33).—"He (St. Augustine)

built also a monastery not far from the same city
(Canterbury), towards the east, in which, by his
advice, Æthelberht built from the foundations the
Church of the Holy Apostles, Peter and Paul, and
enriched it with divers gifts ; in which, also, the
bodies of Augustine himself, of all the bishops of
Canterbury, and likewise of all the kings of Kent
might be buried, which church, however, not Augustine himself, but his successor, Laurentius, consecrated."

This church was consecrated by Laurentius, A.D.
613, and St. Augustine was buried in the north porch
of it (see bk. ii. ch. 3). King Æthelberht and his
Queen Bercta were buried in St. Martin's porch in
it.[1] A second church, dedicated to St. Mary, the
holy mother of God, was built in the same monastery
by Eadbald, King of Kent, and consecrated by Archbishop Mellitus (see bk. ii. ch. 6).

Subsequently, under Abbot Elfnoth, in A.D. 978,
the church was re-dedicated by St. Dunstan in honour
of SS. Peter and Paul and St. Augustine, from whom
the abbey was henceforth called the Monastery of St.
Augustine.   Nothing now remains to tell of the glory
of the church which contained the bones of the first
Archbishops of Canterbury and Kings of Kent except
a few crumbling walls of late Norman date within
the grounds of the Kent and Canterbury Hospital,
outside the walls of the city, a quarter of a mile to
the east of the Cathedral.

[1] Not in the church of St. Martin, although a stone coffin
there is traditionally known as Queen Bercta's tomb ; nor at
Reculver, as we have already pointed out.

The object of building the monastery outside the city appears to have been to allow of a cemetery being attached to it, as the Saxons followed the Romans in forbidding intramural burials. The splendid Norman tower of St. Æthelberht, a drawing of which is preserved in Hasted's "History of Canterbury," was destroyed at the beginning of the present century. A plan of the monastery as it originally existed, with an admirable description by the Rev. Precentor Mackenzie Walcott, will be found in the " Journal of the British Archæological Association " (vol. xxxv. p. 32).

It is not, however, to St. Augustine's Monastery that we wish chiefly to call attention here, but to the remains of the Church of St. Pancras, at the north end of the ancient cemetery, and close to the east side of the Kent and Canterbury Hospital. This church is not mentioned by Bede, but the following tradition concerning it is preserved by William Thorne, a Benedictine monk of St. Augustine's, at the end of the fourteenth century :—

" There was not far from the city (of Canterbury), towards the east, as it were midway between the Church of St. Martin and the walls of the city, a temple or idol house, where King Æthelberht, according to the rites of his tribe, was wont to pray, and with his nobles sacrifice to his demons and not to God ; which temple St. Augustine purged from the filth of the Gentiles; and having broken the image which was in it, changed it into a church, and dedicated it in the name of the martyr St. Pancras, and this was the first church dedicated by St. Augus-

tine. There is still extant an altar in the southern
porticus of the same church, at which the same
Augustine was wont to celebrate, where formerly had
stood the idol of the king ; at which altar, while St.
Augustine was celebrating mass for the first time, the
devil, seeing himself driven out from the home he had
inhabited for long ages, tried to overturn from the
foundations the aforesaid church, the marks of which
are still apparent on the eastern wall of the above-
mentioned porticus."

Excavations have recently been made on the site
of this church, a full description of which is given by
the Rev. Canon C. F. Routledge in the "Archæologia
Cantiana" (vol. xiv. p. 103). It appears that the
church, consisting of a nave, 42 ft. 6 in. by 26 ft.
internally, and a chancel, 31 ft. by 21 ft., is built
upon Roman foundations extending under the nave
and part of the chancel. Upon the west and south
sides of the nave are projecting chambers, measuring
10 ft. 6 in. by 9 ft. 6 in. internally. In the western one
skeletons, protected with stones placed round the body,
were found, and in the southern one a rude altar stone,
4 ft. 4 in. by 4 ft. 2 in. Canon Routledge thinks
this southern chamber may possibly be identified with
the porticus in which St. Augustine celebrated mass
according to Thorne. At the south-east corner of
the nave is the base of a Roman column built into
the brickwork, and at the west end of the nave is a
piece of Roman wall, 9 ft. long and 8 ft. high above
the ground. The Church of St. Pancras was visited
by the British Archæological Association in 1883,
during the Dover Congress, after the foundations had

been laid bare; and Mr. E. P. Loftus Brock, F.S.A., the honorary secretary, in addressing the members present, expressed his opinion that the correctness of the orientation of the Roman foundations, the shape of the plan, with indications of an eastern apse, and the general appearance of the whole pointed to the possibility of its being a relic of a pre-Augustinian Christianity.

During the same congress the Church of St. Martin at Canterbury, was inspected. It is situated outside the city walls, about half a mile east of the Cathedral. The following is an extract from the Rev. Canon Routledge's paper on the subject in the Journal of the Association (vol. xl. p. 47).

"The present outside walls abound in Roman brick; but it had been hitherto supposed that none of the original church was left *in situ*, with the exception, perhaps, of a few fragments in the south wall of the chancel. When, however, about a year and a half ago, we were taking down a portion of the woodwork on the south-east corner of the nave, the whitewash was scraped off underneath and parts of an old wall were exposed to view. This wall was built of stone and rubble, with regular bonding courses of Roman brick at intervals of about nine inches. It was also faced with Roman plastering formed of pounded brick, identical in texture with some brought from the Roman villa at Wigham. This plastering has been traced by me, some four or five feet from the ground, throughout the south side of the nave as far as the baptistery, and on the north side till within a few feet of the western wall. Looking at this and to the average thickness of the walls (about 1 ft. 10 in.), as well as to the discovery, at the beginning of the last century, of a tesselated Roman pavement near the church, I am inclined to hazard the conjecture that the nave was part of an old Roman villa or temple built in the fourth century, and turned into a church, by the addition of the present chancel, at a somewhat later date.

"The chancel is, in great part, built of Roman bricks laid closely and evenly on one another, with no signs of Roman plastering. On its south side two curious openings have been exposed. One is a square doorway, 6 ft. high by 3 ft. 4 in. wide, having a massive lintel of green sandstone, and an equally solid threshold below. This opening had been partially closed up in mediæval times, and used apparently as a low side window. Traces of mediæval wall-painting were found on the later splayed jamb on the west side of the opening. To the east of this is a small semi-circular, arched doorway, the arch being formed of converging blocks of grey sandstone. I am inclined to assign both these openings to Roman workmanship at the end of the fourth century; and we may refer, for the occurrence of square and semi-circular doorways in the same Roman building, to the instance of Jublains, in the department of Mayenne.

"The original church, allowed to fall into partial ruin after the Roman evacuation of Britain, was probably restored, towards the end of the sixth century, to serve as an oratory for Queen Bertha . . . .

"The church consists of a nave, about 38 ft.

long and 25 ft. wide, and a chancel, 39 ft. by 14 ft.'

St. Martin's, the mother-church of England, has certainly strong claims to be considered as of Roman foundation, on account of the distinct historical statement made by Bede, and the partial confirmation it receives from the archæological evidence just detailed; but here, as elsewhere, Christian symbols and burials of the fourth century are wanting to place the age of the building beyond the region of doubt.

Nothing has yet been discovered to prove the truth of Bede's assertion that Canterbury Cathedral was "built by the ancient work of Roman believers." For further information the reader is referred to Dean Stanley's "Memorials of Canterbury"; F. W. Cross's "Rambles round Old Canterbury"; Professor Willis's "Canterbury Cathedral"; and the "Archæologia Cantiana."

The last church in Kent which we shall examine is at Lyminge, six miles north-west of Folkestone, dedicated to St. Mary and St. Eadburg. This place is connected with historical events of great importance in the middle of the seventh century, and it was here that one of the first convents for women was established in England by Queen Æthelburga, who played such a leading part in the conversion of the Northumbrians to Christianity. Æthelburga, the only daughter of Æthelberht, King of Kent and Bertha his Queen, married Ædwin, King of Northumbria, in A.D. 625 (Bede, "Eccl. Hist.," bk. ii. chap. 9), and after the defeat and death of her husband at Hœthfelth, by Penda and Cœdwalla in A.D. 633 (Bede, bk. ii. chap. 20), she was compelled to seek safety in flight. Returning to her native country with Paulinus, she was received with much honour by Honorius, Archbishop of Canterbury, and her brother Eadbald, King of Kent. We learn further, from the writings of the monk Goscelinus (*circa* A.D. 1090) and the charters of the Anglo-Saxon kings, that Queen Æthelburga, vulgarly called St. Eadburg, obtained from her brother, King Eadbald, portion of the park and ville of Lyminge in A.D. 633, and after founding a nunnery, over which she presided as the first Abbess, died there in A.D. 647, being buried on the south side of the present church, which was erected by Dunstan after the dissolution of the Monastery of Lyminge in A.D. 965. The dedication of the first church was to St. Mary, being called in the charter of King Wihtraed, A.D. 697, "Basilica B. Mariæ Genetricis Dei," but it was subsequently dedicated to St. Mary and St. Eadburg.

The ground plan of the present church consists of a nave, with north aisle and west tower, and a chancel. The tower and north aisle were added in the fifteenth century. The greater part of the walls of the chancel and the south wall of the nave are of rude Saxon rubblework. There are round-headed windows, arched with Roman bricks inside, high up in the north and south walls of the chancel, and in the south wall of the nave, and there is a triangular-headed recess at the south-east corner of the nave, also formed of Roman bricks. The rector, the Rev. Canon R. C. Jenkins, has made excavations on the south side of the church, by means of which he has disclosed the existence of a building of Roman workmanship, one wall of which adjoins the south wall of the nave of the present church. The building has an apsidal end, and as its walls are parallel to those of the nave, its orientation is correct. Other remains of Roman walls have been found in the churchyard, showing that an important villa must have existed on the site. Descriptions of the excavations made at Lyminge are given in Mr. C. Roach Smith's "Collectanea Antiqua" (vol. v. p. 185), and in the "Archæologia Cantiana" (vol. x. p. 101). Historical notes about the church, by the Rev. Canon Jenkins, are given in the Journal of the British Archæological Association (vol. xliii. p. 363).

Here, then, as at Reculver and Canterbury, we have a building of undoubted Roman masonry, on an early Saxon Christian site, properly orientated, so that there is nothing very improbable in the suggestion that it may have been used as a place of worship by the pre-Augustinian Christians.

The church at Dover Castle, for which a date in the fourth century has been claimed, although partly built of Roman materials, is clearly of the Saxon period (see J. T. Irvine in "Journal of British Archæological Association," vol. xli. p. 284 ; Sir Gilbert Scott in "Archæologia Cantiana," vol. v. p. 1 ; and the Rev. J. Puckle's "Church and Fortress of Dover Castle"). The evidence as to the existence of christianity in Great Britain during the period of the Roman occupation, which has now been brought forward, is founded on such considerations as the true orientation and general style of the ground-plan of buildings found on sites where Saxon churches are known historically to have been founded, shortly after the landing of St. Augustine on the shores of Kent, with an additional tradition in some cases that a previous place of worship had been erected there by believers in Christ before the departure of the Romans. We propose next to show that more conclusive proofs of the presence of Christians in Britain during the fourth century are afforded by the discovery of Christian symbols in the decorative features of Roman villas.

At the end of the last century a Roman villa with very fine tesselated pavements was found at Frampton, in Dorsetshire, five and a half miles north-west of Dorchester. These remains were thoroughly explored by the great antiquary, Samuel Lysons, and illustrations of the pavements are given in his "Reliquiæ Britannico Romanæ." The largest room in the villa was rectangular, measuring 31 ft. by 21 ft., and had a semicircular apse at one end. Across the apse was a band of ornament composed of a row of seven circles, all filled in with scrolls of foliage, except the centre one, which contained the Chi-Rho monogram of Christ. Immediately adjoining was a head of Neptune, with four dolphins on each side, and a Latin inscription.

Two other Roman pavements found in this country may possibly be Christian,—that at Harpole, in Northamptonshire, which has a circle in the centre divided into eight parts by radial lines, so as to resemble one form of the monogram of Christ ; and that at Horkstow, in Lincolnshire, which has some small red crosses amongst the decorations.[1]

The remains of an extensive Roman villa were discovered at Chedworth, in Gloucestershire,[2] seven miles north of Cirencester, and the objects dug up are preserved in a museum erected on the spot. The Chi-Rho monogram of Christ was found to be carved twice upon one of the foundation-stones of the steps leading into the corridor.

The Chi-Rho monogram, as is generally known, consists of a combination of the first two letters of the name XPICTOC in Greek. The form of this monogram, which occurs at Frampton and at Chedworth, is the earliest and simplest, where the two diagonal strokes of the X cut the lower part of the vertical stroke of the P. In later times various modifications were made by adding a horizontal stroke to the X and by reducing the loop of the P to a mere tail like that of the letter R. The Chi-Rho monogram was first introduced as a Christian symbol by the Emperor Constantine in A.D. 312, the earliest-dated example which has been found in Rome belonging to the year A.D. 323. Its use soon spread from Italy to Gaul, and it exists upon inscribed monuments in the latter country between the years A.D. 377 to 493.[3] The examples found

[1] See T. Morgan's "Romano-British Mosaic Pavements."

[2] "On a Roman Villa at Chedworth," by J. W. Grover, in "Journal of British Archæological Association," vol. xxiv. p. 132.

[3] See Le Blant's "Inscriptions Chrétiennes de la Gaule," and De Rossi's "Christian Inscriptions of Rome."

in Great Britain cannot, therefore, be older than
A.D. 312, when the monogram was first used in Rome,
or later than A.D. 410, when the Romans left this
country, and are probably to be attributed to the
latter half of the fourth century.

Having now completed our survey of the Romano-
British structures, which show traces of Christianity,
we will proceed to examine the sepulchral remains
and monuments of the same period in order to
see how far they confirm the results already
arrived at.

Sepulchral Remains and Monuments.

In conducting the present inquiry as to the possible
existence of a pre-Augustinian Church in Britain, it
is very necessary to be acquainted with the various
points of difference by which a Christian interment
may be distinguished from a pagan one. Almost
every race and every religion has its characteristic
method of disposing of the dead. The Parsees of
Persia expose the bodies of their departed relations
in "towers of silence," to be devoured by birds of
prey; and some Indian tribes of North America place
the deceased in a wooden coffin, which is set afloat
on one of the great freshwater lakes to be carried
away by the wind to the happy hunting-ground; but
in Europe the dead are invariably returned to the
mother-earth from which they originally sprang.
"Dust thou art, to dust shalt thou return." The
three principal ways of treating the body previous to
burial are by embalming, the object of which is to
prevent decay; by cremation, which reduces the

whole to ashes ; and by swathing it in grave clothes without any attempt being made to arrest or accelerate the processes of natural decomposition. Interments may also be classified according to the character of the excavation or structure prepared for the reception of the dead. The pre-historic man in some cases made use of natural caves in the rock as a burial place, and the Catacombs are examples of artificial caves excavated for the same purpose. The simplest and most common method of interment is to dig a grave in the earth in which the coffin or funeral urn is placed, with or without some masonry structure to protect it. Mound burial is more elaborate, a large heap of earth being raised above the grave or chamber in which the body is contained. Lastly, the bones of the deceased may be deposited in a stone coffin above ground, a method that can, perhaps, hardly be called burial.

Special forms of religious belief and superstition have led to the practice of placing various objects used by the living in the tombs of the dead. Thus there are three chief points to be noticed in discriminating between sepulchral remains of individuals of different races and different religious beliefs : (1) the way of treating the body before burial ; (2) the character of the excavation or structure prepared for its reception, and (3) the nature of the objects placed in the grave with it. In the case of Christian interments, also the position of the body as regards its orientation must be observed.

Mr. E. P. Loftus Brock, in his paper on the "Evidences of the Extent of the Ancient British

Church" in the "Journal of the British Archæological Association" (vol. xli. p. 53), mentions a cemetery beneath Bishopsgate Street in London, on the Roman level, where the bodies lie east and west, and are unaccompanied by any Pagan objects.

A very good general description of the Roman modes of sepulture in Britain is to be found in the late Mr. Thomas Wright's "The Celt, Roman, and the Saxon" (chap. x.), and his "Uriconium"; and numerous examples are illustrated in Mr. C. Roach Smith's "Collectanea Antiqua"; also a few in Mr. M. H. Bloxam's "Companion to Gothic Architecture." Amongst most civilised nations the place of interment of the dead is marked by a monument with symbolic or other figure sculpture and a commemorative inscription. The best illustrations of Romano-British sepulchral monuments are given in Dr. J. Collingwood Bruce's "Lapidarium Septentrionale," and John Horsley's "Britannia Romana."

With regard to the method of treating the body before burial employed by the Romans, Mr. Thomas Wright gives the following particulars :—"We learn from the ancient writers that it was the earlier practice of the Romans to bury the body of their dead entire ; and it was not until the time of the dictator Scylla, that the custom of burning the dead was established. From this time either usage continued to be adopted, at the will of the individual, or of the family of the deceased ; but, in the second century of the Christian era, the older practice is said to have become again more fashionable than that of cremation, and from this time gradually superseded it. We find that both modes of burial were used indiscriminately in Roman Britain, and it is probable that the different people who composed the Roman population adopted that practice which was most agreeable to their own prejudices. The practice of burning the dead and burying the ashes in urns seems, however, to have predominated."

The difference between the Christian and Pagan methods of treating the body before burial amongst the Romans was that, whilst the Pagans partially adopted cremation, the Christians never did so. Our knowledge of Christian Roman modes of sepulture is derived almost exclusively from the Catacombs at Rome. Here the body was either placed in a coffin hollowed out of the solid rock, and closed with a marble or terra-cotta slab bearing an epitaph or symbols of our faith, or it was enclosed in a massive stone sarcophagus sculptured with scenes from Scripture. The custom of burying objects with the deceased, such as vessels, lachrymatories, and lamps, and placing a coin in his mouth to pay for ferrying the soul across the Styx in Charon's boat, ceased with the introduction of Christianity, except in the case of the remarkable survival of paganism, where a bishop has his crozier, &c., placed in his coffin. As the Christians never burned their dead, it will be unnecessary here to describe the various ways in which the Romans disposed of the urns containing cremated human bones, and we will pass on at once to the sepulture of entire bodies. All the Roman cemeteries were, according to their earliest code of laws, invariably situated outside the walls of the large cities.

Extramural cemeteries of the Roman period have been discovered in this country at London, Colchester, and York, where a representative series of specimens, showing the different methods of burial, has been admirably arranged in the Museum by the Rev. Canon Raine.

When the body was buried entire it was generally placed in a coffin of wood, lead, or stone, filled with liquid quicklime. The wooden coffins have in all cases rotted away, but their original existence has been inferred by the presence of quantities of iron nails found near the skeleton. The leaden coffins are often ornamented with scollop-shells and bead-mouldings interspersed with small circles, but in no case has any Christian symbol been noticed upon them. The stone sarcophagi were either very massive and plain, like most of those at York, or with a panel bearing an inscription on one side, like that of Simplicia Florentina in the York Museum, or ornamented with a sculptured bust of the deceased, like the one dug up in Haydon Square, London, and now in the British Museum. Both the ornament and the inscriptions are, in all the specimens which have as yet been discovered, of a purely Pagan type, with the exception of the sarcophagus of Valerius Amandinus in the Chapter House of Westminster Abbey. The lid of this sarcophagus has a cross upon it, but in all probability the Christian symbol was added at a later period. Shortly after the discovery of the sarcophagus in 1869, the late Dean Stanley read a paper on the subject before the British Archæological Institute (see Proceedings, vol. xxvii.), and the question of the

date of the cross on the lid was fully discussed.   It
was generally admitted that the cross could not be of
Roman origin, and might possibly be as late as the
twelfth century.   The following passage from Bede's
"Ecclesiastical History" (book iv. ch. 19) gives a
curious instance of a Roman sarcophagus being re-
used in Saxon times: "When she (St. Etheldreda)
had been buried sixteen years, the same abbess
(Sexburg) thought fit that her bones should be taken
up, and, having been put in a new coffin, should be
transferred into the church; and she ordered certain of the brethren to seek for a stone of which
they might make a coffin for this purpose; and they,
having gone on board a ship (for this same region of
Ely is on every side encompassed by waters and
swamps, and has no large stones), came to a certain
desolate little city, situate not far from thence, which is
called in the tongue of the Angles, Grantchester; and
presently they found, close to the walls of the city, a
coffin beautifully wrought of white marble, and covered
also most exactly with a lid of the same kind of stone."

A Roman sarcophagus was discovered some years
ago at Hartlip in Kent, with two palm branches
carved upon it, which Mr. C. Roach Smith[1] believes
to be Christian, as this symbol does not occur in
connection with Pagan interments.

A large number of Romano-British sepulchral
monuments have been discovered from time to time
in this country outside the walls of the great cities,
such as York, Cirencester, Lincoln, Bath, Colchester,

[1] "Collectanea Antiqua," vol. i. p. 183.

Wroxeter, and London. The best collections are to be seen in the museums at Newcastle-on-Tyne, Chester, and Caerleon. These monuments consist of blocks of stone, generally of much larger size than those used in later times for the same purpose, varying in height from 5 ft. to 7 ft., and in breadth from 2 ft. 6 in. to 3 ft., being evidently intended to be placed in an erect position over the grave. The stone was usually sculptured on the front only with a bas-relief representing the deceased as a soldier on horseback, or as a female seated on a chair. The commonest shape for the tombstone was rectangular, with a pedimented top. The inscription either occupied the whole of the face of the stone or was enclosed in a panel beneath the bas-relief. The letters used are Roman capitals, and many of the words are expressed by contractions. The prefix D. M., or Diis Manibus,—that is, "to the gods of the shades," occurs in almost all Roman Pagan epitaphs, or, occasionally, D. M. S., equivalent to Diis Manibus Sacris ("to the sacred gods of the shades"). Then comes the name of the deceased, his age expressed thus, for example: "vixit annos xxxv menses viii dies xv" (lived thirty-five years, eight months, fifteen days), although in most cases the number of years only is given. Next, the name of the erector of the monument and his or her relation to the deceased, often with the addition of some tender epithet. The word used for erected is either "fecit" (made this), or "faciendum curarit" (caused to be made), or "posuit" (placed this). The name of the erector is not always given, but instead "heredes F. C." (his heirs caused this to be made). The epitaphs terminate with the letters H. S. E., the contraction for "hic situs est" (he is placed here), or "hic sepultus est" (here he is buried). The occupation of the deceased is sometimes given, but the date of his death is never mentioned.

Let us now compare the Roman Pagan epitaphs with the Christian ones of the same period in the Catacombs of Rome, a good description of which will be found in the Rev. Canon J. S. Northcote's book on the subject. The chief characteristic of the earliest Christian sepulchral inscriptions is their shortness and simplicity, often nothing beyond the name of the deceased being given. The D. M. of Pagan times is discarded; instead, we have pious acclamations, such as "Vivas in Deo, in Christo, in Domino, in Pace, cum Sanctis," &c., accompanied by distinctly Christian symbols, such as the Chi-Rho monogram, the dove with the olive branch, the dolphin, the anchor, &c.

The age of the deceased often occurs in the inscriptions expressed in years, months, days, and even hours, together with the day of the month, but not the year when his death took place.

Canon Brownlow, in his "Epitaphs of the Catacombs" (chap. v.), contrasts the Pagan and Christian ideas with regard to death in the following passage :—"Out of the innumerable monumental inscriptions of Pagan Rome which have reached us, we have sought in our last chapter to gather as clear an idea as we could of the notions entertained by their authors as to the existence of a future state ;

and we have seen that not one affirms it, though the hearts of many manifestly yearned for it. Affectionate hearts could not bear to think that they were hopelessly and eternally separated from those whom they had loved so truly when alive ; and with hesitating tongue, therefore, and in images borrowed from poetry, they call upon the inexorable Manes to deal mercifully with the departed, or to take compassion upon the survivors, and to bring back the image of the beloved in dreams and visions of the night. The Christian inscriptions, on the other hand, imply, even when they do not actually express, a firm belief in the reality of a future life ; they pray for the dead as though still living, and capable of feeling joy and sorrow ; or they call upon them for assistance as though they were still able to give it ; and often the very language in which they speak of death and all that concerns it bears with it an unconscious testimony to the faith in a future resurrection."

Up to the present time no Romano - British sepulchral monument has been discovered, which can either by the formula of its inscription or the symbols upon it be proved to be Christian, unless the stone at Llanerfil be an instance, on account of its bearing the epitaph in Latin capitals : " Hic in tumulo jacit Restice filia Paternini an xiii in pa(ce)." The formula " in pace " is very common in the epitaphs of the Catacombs during the first four centuries.

We shall next consider the portable objects of the Romano-British period which can lay claim to be Christian.

Portable Objects.

In dealing with the portable objects of Roman manufacture discovered in this country, it must not be forgotten that some of them may possibly have been imported from abroad long after the fourth century, and therefore any evidence as to the existence of Christianity in Great Britain before that time founded on the discovery of such objects must necessarily fall to the ground.

Lists of Christian objects of Roman manufacture found in Great Britain have been compiled by Messrs. Haddon and Stubbs[1] and Æmilius Hübner[2] and a few more examples have been brought to light since, but the total number at present known to exist is exceedingly small when compared with the vast quantity of relics which have been dug up on the sites of Romano-British towns, villas, and cemeteries.

The Chi-Rho monogram occurs on the following objects of Roman manufacture found in Great Britain, thus proving them to be Christian.

Two cakes of pewter found in the Thames at Battersea, and now in the British Museum ("Proc. Soc. Ant. Lond.," vol. ii. 2nd ser. p. 234).

A silver bowl found in 1736 at Corbridge, in Northumberland, now lost, but a drawing of which has been preserved (Dr. J. Collingwood Bruce's "Lapidarium Septentrionale," p. 342).

A leaden seal found in 1872 in a room on the south

---

[1] "Councils and Ecclesiastical Documents," edited after Spelman and Wilkins, and published 1869.

[2] "Inscriptiones Britanniæ Christianæ," 1876.

side of the Forum at Silchester, in Hampshire ("Archæologia," vol. xlvi. p. 363).

Two silver rings found on the site of a Roman villa at Fifehead Neville, in Dorsetshire ("Proc. Soc. Ant. Lond.," vol. ix. 2nd series, p. 68).

Doubtful instances of the Chi-Rho monogram also occur on a small vessel of red Caistor ware in the Duke of Northumberland's Museum at Alnwick, in Northumberland (Dr. Collingwood Bruce's Catalogue, p. 9), and on a bronze foot-rule in the York Museum.[1]

A piece of Samian ware found at Catterick Bridge, in Yorkshire, and now in the possession of Sir Wilfrid Lawson, marked with a cross ("Journ. Brit. Archæol. Inst.," vol. vi. p. 81), and two pieces of Roman tile in the Cirencester Museum, having the letters I.H.S. upon them ("Journ. Brit. Archæol. Assoc.," vol. xxiii., p. 226), are also of doubtful authenticity.

The Christian formula VIVAS IN DEO occurs on two Roman gold rings, one found at Brancaster, in Norfolk, in 1829 ("Archæologia," vol. xxiii. p. 361), and the other found at Silchester, in Hampshire, in 1786 ("Archæologia," vol. viii. p. 449).

This concludes the very meagre list of Roman objects discovered in Great Britain which have any claim to be considered as of Christian origin.

The general outcome of the investigations pursued in the foregoing chapter tends to show that neither in the structures, the sepulchral remains, nor the portable objects of the Romano-British period are sufficient traces of Christianity apparent to justify

---

[1] The supposed monogram seemed to me to be only part of the divisions of the rule, when I examined it.

the belief that any appreciable proportion of the inhabitants of this country had been reclaimed from paganism before the end of the fourth century. The late Mr. Thomas Wright, whose opinion is entitled to considerable weight, comes to the same conclusion in his "The Celt, Roman, and Saxon," and shows that at all events the legendary stories, such as the one about Lucius, King of the Britons, writing to Pope Eleuthenius in A.D. 156, are entirely at variance with the results arrived at by archæological research. He thinks also that the supposed historical statement as to the presence of British bishops at Arles in A.D. 314 does not rest on sufficiently reliable authority to be accepted without further confirmation, and that the general allusions made by Tertullian, Origen, Jerome, and other early Christian writers as to the existence of a Romano-British Church, " must evidently be taken as little better than flourishes of rhetoric."

A less sceptical view of the case is held by Mr. J. W. Grover, F.S.A., in his paper on " Pre-Augustinian Christianity in Great Britain," and Mr. E. P. Loftus Brock, F.S.A., in his paper on the "Evidences of the extent of the Ancient British Church" (see "Journal of the British Archæological Institute," vol. xxiii. p. 221, and vol. xli. p. 53).

CHAPTER II.

THE ARCHÆOLOGY OF THE PRE-AUGUSTINIAN OR EARLY CELTIC CHURCH (A.D. 400-600).

Structures.

Soon after the Romans left Britain the Saxon invasions began, and there is a period of nearly 200 years previous to the landing of St. Augustine on the shores of Kent, during which the non-Celtic portions of this country were dominated by Northern paganism. It would be useless, therefore, to seek for Christian remains of the fifth and sixth centuries in any part of England except the extreme west, and it is to Ireland, Scotland, and Wales that we must chiefly now direct our attention. All traces of the buildings of this early period have disappeared in Wales and Cornwall, but in Ireland and Scotland the case is different, as the remoteness and inaccessibility of the sites chosen by the first missionaries for their monastic settlements have been the means of preserving intact to the present day the most primitive type of Christian Church now existing in any part of Europe. There is nothing in the ecclesiastical buildings of Wales or Cornwall to indicate any great antiquity, except the simplicity of the ground-plan and the rudeness of the masonry. Probably none of them are older than the eleventh century, and all are built with mortar.

The chief proof of the great age of the oldest

churches in Ireland and Scotland is that there is no break in the continuity of style between methods of construction employed by the Pagan and the Christian Celts. Irish ecclesiastical architecture was developed out of the Pagan architecture which preceded it, but the structures were specialised by being orientated and otherwise adapted to the ritual of the newly-introduced religion and the requirements of the monastic community. That the inhabitants of certain portions of Great Britain had attained considerable proficiency in the art of masonry construction at a very early period, is proved by the great stone fortresses of the west of Ireland, the Pictish towers of the north of Scotland, and the tumuli with domed roofs of which there are such splendid examples at Maeshowe in Orkney, and Newgrange, county Meath. The chief peculiarity of these structures is the absence of the use of cement and the entire ignorance of the principle of the arch. The want of mortar is made up for by the large size of the stones, and the careful way in which they are fitted together and wedged up with smaller stones between the joints, so that many of these dry-built structures have outlived the more recent buildings by several centuries. Ignorance of the principle of the arch led to the sloping jambs of the doorways, in order to lessen the space to be spanned by the lintel, and to the ingenious double lintel to take the pressure off the lower one and serving the same purpose as the relieving arch of a later style. All these peculiar features will be noticed in the Christian buildings we are about to describe.

Lord Dunraven, in his splendid work on Irish architecture, illustrates eight of the Pagan forts or cathairs on the three islands of Aran and five in the counties of Sligo and Kerry. The finest of these are Dun Aengus or Aranmôr, Dun Conor on the middle island of Aran, and Staic Fort county Kerry. The latter has its doorway with the double lintel and reveal for a wooden door still in perfect preservation. The stone forts of Ireland are found chiefly on the west coast, in the counties of Kerry, Clare, Galway, and Sligo. They are generally either circular or oval in shape, varying in internal diameter from 75 ft. to 200 ft., having walls from 12 ft. to 18 ft. thick at the base, and 15 ft. to 20 ft. high, with a series of steps running up and down all round the inside, in order to give access to the platforms at various levels formed by the offsets. Within the area enclosed by the walls of the fort there is in most cases a bee-hive hut, an underground chamber, or some other structure. The defensive outworks consist of additional exterior walls and chevaux-de-frise of stones scattered in all directions, to impede the advance of an attacking party. The doorways, which seldom exceed one in number, are from 5 ft. to 6 ft. wide with lintels and reveals for a door.

The brochs or Pictish towers of the north of Scotland have so many points in common with the Irish cathairs as regards the methods of construction employed, that it seems probable that they were built either by the same race, or at all events by a people in the same stage of civilisation. The origin of the brochs has been thoroughly investigated by Dr.

Joseph Anderson in the "Archæologia Scotica" (vol. vii.), in the "Proceedings" of the Society of Antiquaries of Scotland, and in his "Rhind Lectures on Scotland in Pagan Times"; and these structures are believed by him to have been erected in the two or three centuries immediately before the introduction of Christianity into this country. It is probable, therefore, that the Irish cathairs belong to the same period. The only stone forts in other parts of Great Britain that can in any way be compared with those of Scotland or Ireland are found in North Wales, the finest specimen being on the summit of Tr'r Ceiri, in Caernarvonshire. History throws no light on the probable age of these Pagan stone forts; but in Ireland they are associated with the names of Aengus, Conor, and other mythical heroes of Firbolg race, whose adventures are related in the Books of Lecan and Ballymote.

Whenever a new religion has been introduced into any country it has been either by conquest or with the sanction of the governing power. Ireland was Christianised by peaceful means, and the first missionaries began by converting the reigning chieftains, from whom they afterwards received such protection as enabled them to preach to the people without molestation. In the state of society which existed in Ireland when the greater part of the population was still Pagan, it was absolutely necessary that the priests should have some fortified place where they could retire for safety in case of sudden attack or outbreak of fanatical violence. After the king or chieftain of each province had been baptized, the saint by whom he was converted generally asked and obtained permission to build his first church within the royal dun or fortress. Historical instances of this are recorded in the lives of St. Patrick, St. Bennen, and St. Caillin (see Petrie's "Ecclesiastical Architecture of Ireland," pp. 161 and 446). One of the first churches erected by St. Patrick in the county of Meath was that of Donaghpatrick near Tailteann (now Teltown), on the north bank of the Blackwater, between Navan and Kells. We are told in the "Tripartite Life of St. Patrick," and also in the life of the same saint in the Book of Armagh, that Conall MacNeill, brother of Laoghaire, King of Meath, gave up his house in order to provide a site. There is still to be seen near the church a great rath, or earthwork, with four ramparts and ditches, which Sir William Wild considers to be one of the finest of the kind in Ireland (see the "Boyne and the Blackwater"). The church was 60 ft. long, and Conall MacNeill gave the site for the God of Patrick, measuring the length with his own feet.

When St. Patrick founded Armagh the chieftain Daire said to him: "I will not give that [the site on the high ground called Ardd Mache] to thee, but I will give thee a place for thy church in the strong rath below, where Da Ferta [the two graves] are." With regard to the dimensions of this monastic establishment we are told in the "Tripartite Life" that "The way in which St. Patrick made the Fertæ was this, seven score feet in the Less (or Fort), and seven-and-twenty feet in the Tigh Mor (or Great House), and seventeen feet in the Cuile (or kitchen), and seven feet in the Aregal (or Oratory). And it was thus that the houses of the Conghail (the churches) were built always." [1]

It is related in the Life of St. Bennen, published by Colgan in his "Trias Thaumaturga," that the church of Cill Benen was built by St. Patrick, within the Dun of the chieftain Lughaidh, who was baptized with his father and four brothers. When Dr. Petrie visited Kilbannon, near Tuam, county Galway, in 1826, the remains of this great rath were visible; but since that time all traces have disappeared. We learn also from the Life of St. Caillin, in the "Book of Fenagh," that Aohd Finn, the son of Feargua, chieftain of Breifny, after his conversion by St. Caillen, allowed a monastery to be established in his cathair,[2] or fortress, of which vestiges still exist. The truth of these historical statements is fully borne out by the archæological evidence, which has been so assiduously collected by Dr. Petrie, Lord Dunraven, Miss Margaret Stokes, R. Rolt Brash, and others. The remains of early churches associated with Pagan raths in Ireland have been very carefully examined and described,

[1] Todd's "Life of St. Patrick," p. 477. In the "Annals of the Four Masters" under the date A.D. 1092, the ecclesiastical establishment at Armagh is called "the *Rath* of Armagh, with its churches." See also Whitley Stokes's "Tripartite Life of St. Patrick," Rolls series.

[2] The word "Cathair," or "Caiseal," is usually employed in ancient Irish to signify a stone fort, and the term "Rath" or "Lis" is applied to an earthwork, "Dun" being used indiscriminately to mean either. The wall surrounding the early monasteries in Ireland was in the first instance erected for purposes of defence, but in later times it was only kept up in order to ensure greater seclusion from the world outside.

but although many similar instances are to be found in Wales, not much attention has hitherto been bestowed upon the matter.[1] With regard to the existence of churches within fortified enclosures in Scotland, Dr. Joseph Anderson remarks in his "Rhind Lectures on Scotland in Early Christian Times" (1st series, p. 93) :—"I cannot, however, point to a single example in this country (Scotland) so typical as those that have been described (in Ireland); but if I were to conclude from my inability to do so, that such groups never existed, I should commit the common mistake of drawing from mere ignorance of the facts a conclusion which could only be legitimately drawn from complete knowledge. I rather incline to the opinion founded on my opinion of how very little we do know of the real character of the vast majority of the great stone cashels and earthen raths of Scotland, that there may be found among them some which exhibit distinct and complete evidence of this Christian character."

On the islands off the west coast of Ireland there are several early monastic settlements situated within stone forts, the best preserved specimens being those on Skellig Mhichel, on Ardoilean, on Oilen Tsenaig, on Inisglora, and on Inismurray.

Skellig Mhichel is one of two rocky islands situated eight miles off Bolus Head, the south-west

---

[1] A great number of the churches in South Wales are situated in close proximity to Pagan raths. This is especially the case in Pembrokeshire, as may be seen by consulting the Ordnance Map. Caerau Church, near Cardiff, takes its name from a caer, or earthwork, still existing.

promontory of the county of Kerry, and known as
the Great and Little Skellig, access to which can be
obtained by boat from either Valencia or Waterville
(Ordnance Map, 1 inch scale, sheet 190).

The Great Skellig is also called Skellig Mhichel on
account of the church upon it being dedicated to St.
Michael, the patron saint of high places, who gives
his name to similar rocks off the coasts of Normandy
and Cornwall. There are two lighthouses upon the
south end of Skellig Mhichel, which help to warn
ships off its treacherous shores.[1] The island is a huge
pyramidal mass of rock, the horizontal lines of the
stratification of which indicate a peaceful origin in long
past geological ages, but now, war with the elements
for centuries, has scarred its surface and riven it
in all directions. The wild waves of the Atlantic
beat unceasingly against its precipitous cliffs, dashing
themselves to pieces and falling back in white foam.
Skellig Mhichel is a veritable desert in the ocean,
such as Adamnan tells us that Columba retired to
when he wished to commune with God alone.

Here, surrounded by a vast waste of sea, with the
blue sky above and disturbed by no sound save the
cry of the sea-birds, the early Irish saints perfected
that life of self-denial, and attained that high spiritual
excellence, which is only possible to those who retire
for at least a season from the cares of the world.
Some lived and died in this ocean solitude, but
others reaped the reward of their own self-sacrifice
and that of their companions, when they spread the

---

[1] One is 173 ft. above high water and the other 372 ft.

bright light of Christianity throughout Europe in the seventh and eighth centuries.

Skellig Mhichel rises from the sea in two peaks, the higher one being at the southern end of the island. The Church of St. Michael, with its group of monastic cells, is situated near the summit of the northern peak, which is lower and more rounded in form than the other. The landing-place is at the north end of the island, and a zigzag road leads up from it along the face of the cliff on the east side, to the lighthouse. The lower part of the ancient approach to the church from the landing-place, which was on the north-east side of the island, has been broken away; but the upper part, consisting of 620 steps up the slope from the valley between the two peaks in a northerly direction, still remains. The ascent is now made, partly by the zigzag road constructed by the workmen of the lighthouse, up to a point in the valley just mentioned, 120 ft. above sea level, and the remainder of the way by the ancient flight of steps.

"The island has been the scene of annual pilgrimages for many centuries, and the service of the 'Way of the Cross' is still celebrated here, though with some perfectly traditional forms of prayer and customs, such as are now only found to exist among the islanders along the west coast of Ireland."[1]

The "Way of the Cross" is up the flight of steps on which there are three stations, or resting-places, "Christ's Saddle," or the Garden of the Passion; the

[1] Lord Dunraven's "Notes on Irish Architecture," vol. i. p. 30.

E

"Stone of Pain," where is commemorated the moment when Our Lord, bowed under the weight of the Cross, sank to the ground; the "Rock of Woman's Wailing," where the words of Christ on his walk to Calvary are recalled,—"Daughters of Jerusalem, weep not for me, but weep for yourselves and your children."

The monastic settlement is reached at the top of the flight of steps already mentioned, and the entrance is through a door in the wall of the Cashel. The group of buildings are placed on a sort of plateau, just below the summit of the northern point of the island, measuring 180 ft. long by 100 ft. wide. On the west, or land-side it is bounded by the cliff which rises up behind it, and on the east side next the sea it is surrounded by a dry built wall with a face having a curved batter, like that at Staigue Fort, county Kerry.

"It is astonishing to conceive the courage and skill of the builders of this fine wall, placed as it is on the very edge of the precipice, at a vast height above the sea, with no standing ground outside the wall from which the builders could have worked; yet the face is as perfect as that of Staigue Fort."[1]

The group of structures within the Cashel consists of St. Michael's Church (a building of later date than the rest constructed with mortar); two stone-roofed oratories; six bee-hive huts (one of which is in ruins); two wells; and five "leachta," or burial-places. The bee-hive huts are all dry-built, and exactly of the same type as the "clochauns" within the Pagan fort of

[1] Lord Dunraven's "Notes on Irish Architecture," vol. i., p. 28.

Dun Bec, county Kerry.[1] They are circular in plan externally, ranging in diameter from 15 to 25 ft., and rectangular within, the smallest measuring 7 ft. by 7 ft., and the largest 15 ft. by 12 ft.; the walls are from 4 ft. to 6 ft. thick; the height of the largest cell inside is 16 ft. 6 in., and the smallest 12 ft. The side walls are vertical for about half their height internally, above which the stones are made to overlap so as to form a dome of bee-hive shape externally. The openings consist of a single door with sloping jambs from 3 ft. 6 in. to 4 ft. 6 in. high, from 2 ft. to 3 ft. wide at the bottom, and from 1 ft. 6 in. to 2 ft. 6 in. wide at the top; one or two small windows near the roof from 1 ft. to 1 ft. 6 in. square; and a hole in the top of the dome. The floors of the cells are paved and divided into one or two steps. In the interior there are three recesses or cupboards in the wall 2 ft. high by 1 ft. 6 in. wide, and double rows of projecting stone pegs, intended possibly for hanging up book satchels and other objects. The largest cell has several stones projecting from its domed roof on the outside, and two set-offs in the wall. The doors of two of the cells have double lintels, thus exactly resembling in construction the entrance to Staigue Fort, county Kerry, already described. Just above the window over the doorway of the largest cell is a cross composed of six white quartz pebbles, which appear very distinctly by contrast with the dark colour of the slate stone of the rest of the wall. A similar cross occurs over the doorway of one of the

[1] Lord Dunraven's "Notes on Irish Architecture," vol. i. p. 21.

oratories on Oilen Tsenaig, Magharee Islands, county Kerry.

It will not be necessary to notice the Church of St. Michael on the Great Skellig, as it is built with mortar, and, therefore, being of later date than the other structures, does not come within the scope of our present inquiry.

There are two oratories in the monastic settlement on Skellig Mhichel, one surrounded by the six cells just described, and the other a short distance to the northward. The first of these is rectangular in ground-plan both inside and out, measuring 10 ft. by 6 ft. internally, and having walls from 3 ft. to 4 ft. thick. The roof is constructed like those of the cells with stones overlapping so as to form an oval dome. The only openings are a doorway with sloping jambs, at one end 4 ft. 10 in. high, 3 ft. 8 in. wide at the bottom, and 3 ft. 2 in. wide at the top; and a small window at the other, 1 ft. 6 in. high, by 1 ft. 3 in. wide externally. The building is not properly orientated, but faces north-east. It has a rude altar platform under the window, opposite the door, raised above the level of the rest of the floor. The second oratory, which stands alone apart from the cells, is like the first rectangular in ground-plan both inside and out, measuring 8 ft. by 6 ft. internally, and having walls. The roof is formed like that of the Oratory of Gallerus, county Kerry. The stones overlap each other, but the corners and sides of the rectangular ground-plan are preserved up to the top of the structure, instead of dying off into an oval dome. The openings consist of a doorway with sloping jambs, 3 ft. 6 in.

high, 1 ft. 10 in. wide at the bottom, and 1 ft. 8 in. at the top; and a small window facing it at the opposite end, 2 ft. wide and 1 ft. high. The second oratory is more correctly orientated than the first, but has its longer axis still a little north of east.

The first historical notice of an ecclesiastical settlement on Skellig Mhichel is under the year A.D. 823, when the monastery was plundered by the Danes, and Eitgall taken prisoner; but, whatever may be the exact age of the group of structures we have just described, the type is the very earliest it will be possible to find, because it belongs to the transition period between paganism and Christianity.

Except for the cross over the doorway of the largest cell, there is nothing by which the domestic buildings on Skellig Mhichel can be distinguished from the Pagan clochauns, within the fort at Dun Bec, county Kerry, and the same constructive peculiarities, such as the sloping jambs, double lintels, absence of cement, and ignorance of the principle of the arch, are found both here and in the Staigue Fort, county Kerry.

The two oratories on Skellig Mhichel exhibit features which show that, although the Irish missionaries adopted the style of architecture already existing in the country for the houses in which they lived, it was necessary to introduce certain modifications into the buildings used for places of worship, so as to adapt them to the ritual and requirements of Celtic Christianity. The differences between the bee-hive cells in which the monks lived and oratories in which they performed their devotions are that, instead of being circular, the oratories are rectangular in ground-plan, both inside and out; that they are properly orientated with a door at the west end, and a small window facing it at the east end; and that there is a platform raised above the level of the floor at the east end for an altar. It was thus that a native style of eeclesiastical architecture was gradually developed in Ireland, and the origin of the oratory may be traced back to the clochaun. In Italy the earliest churches were copied from the Roman basilica with its apsidal end, but in Ireland the semi-circular apse is entirely unknown. The Irish monastic settlements differed from those of the Western Church of later times in having a large number of separate cells for the monks instead of one common dormitory. This practice may perhaps have come from the East, as many similar monasteries formerly existed in the deserts of the Thebaid, of which notices have been preserved.[1]

It will not be necessary to describe in detail the other groups of monastic buildings within stone cashels found on the west coast of Ireland, but the following short notes on the most important ones may prove useful.

On Ardoilean, or High Island, three miles off the west coast of co. Galway, just south of Inisboffin, is a circular cashel, 108 ft. in diameter inside, enclosing a church 12 ft. by 10 ft. inside, with a cross on the lintel of the doorway, two large bee-hive cells, and

[1] Sir Gilbert Scott's "Lectures on Architecture," vol. ii. p. 20. The Carthusian monks still sleep in separate cells, like the ancient Irish.

several smaller ones. The settlement is supposed to have been founded by St. Fechin, abbot of Fore, who died A.D. 664 (Petrie's "Ancient Architecture of Ireland," p. 424; and Kinahan, in "Proc. of Royal Irish Academy," vol. x. p. 551).

On Inismurray, off the coast of co. Sligo, between Sligo and Galway Bays, is a splendid cashel in good preservation, of irregular oval shape, measuring 175 ft. by 135 ft. inside, with a wall 15 ft. high and 13 ft. broad, enclosing three dry-built bee-hive cells; three churches built with cement, one of very small dimensions, 9 ft. by 8 ft. inside, with a stone roof and cross on the lintel of the doorway, dedicated to St. Molaise; and several leachtas, &c. The earliest mention of Inismurray in the Irish Annals is under the year A.D. 747 (Lord Dunraven's "Notes on Irish Architecture," vol. i. p. 45; and W. F. Wakeman in "Jour. Royal Hist. and Archæol. Assoc. of Ireland," vol. vii., 4th series, p. 175).

On Oilen Tsenaig, or St. Senach's Island, one of the Magharees, off the coast of Kerry, outside Tralee Bay, is a circular cashel, 150 ft. diameter inside, with a wall 18 ft. thick, enclosing three bee-hive cells; two small dry-built oratories, one 14 ft. by 9 ft. inside, with a domed roof of overlapping stones; and three leachtas (Lord Dunraven's "Notes on Irish Architecture," vol. i. p. 37).

On Inisglora, one mile off the north-west coast of co. Sligo, are the remains of a cashel, enclosing three bee-hive cells; three churches, one a dry-built, stone-roofed oratory, measuring 12 ft. by 8 ft. 6 in. inside, dedicated to St. Brendan, and the other two of later

date built with cement; some leachta, and a holy
well with a stone roof. St. Brendan, the founder of
this monastery, died A.D. 484 (Lord Dunraven's
"Notes on Irish Architecture," vol. i. p. 40).

Dr. Joseph Anderson, in his "Scotland in Early
Christian Times,"[1] thus summarises the characteristic
features of the earliest type of Christian remains in
Ireland :—

(1) "That they exist as composite groups, compris-
ing one or more churches placed in association with
monastic dwellings, which consist of dry-built cells of
bee-hive shape, the whole settlement being enclosed
within a cashel or rampart of uncemented stones;
(2) that the churches found in this association are
invariably of small size and rude construction; (3)
that whether they are lime-built with perpendicular
walls, or dry built and roofed like the dwellings, by
bringing the walls gradually together, they are always
rectangular on ground plan, and single chambered;
(4) they have usually a west doorway and always an
east window over the altar."

Examples of Christian settlements of this class,
which originated first in Ireland, have been found in
Scotland on an island in Loch Columkille, in Skye;
on Eilean na Naoimh, one of the Garveloch Islands,
lying between Scarba and Mull; and on the Brough
of Deerness in Orkney. These most interesting remains are described in Dr. J. Anderson's admirable
course of Rhind Lectures, and therefore as they possess no special peculiarities which have not been
already mentioned when dealing with the Irish parent-

[1] First Series, p. 92.

structures, it will be unnecessary to do more than refer the reader for further information to Dr. Anderson's work and T. S. Muir's "Ecclesiological Notes on some of the islands of Scotland."

Besides the monastic establishments, consisting of a group of structures within a cashel, there are several examples of early dry-built churches of small size, both in Ireland and Scotland, in isolated positions, without any cells or enclosing wall. It will be necessary to mention some of these, as their structural details enable us to trace still further the evolution of some of the most striking peculiarities of Irish architecture.

It has been already pointed out that the structures on Skellig Mhichel, used for purposes of worship, differed from the dwelling-houses in being rectangular in ground-plan both inside and outside, instead of being rectangular within and circular without. In the first stage of transition, from the bee-hive cell to the rectangular stone-roofed oratory, although the side walls had square corners, the dome at the top was still oval, but in the next stage the square angle was carried up to the level of the ridge which ran in the direction of the long axis of the building.

The best specimen of this latter type of structure is the Oratory of Gallerus, near Dingle, in the county Kerry. It is most beautifully constructed of flat greenstone rubble put together without mortar and carefully dressed to the curve of the roof. The excellence of the workmanship is such that the stones have held together without cement of any kind for perhaps a thousand years, and the whole is perfectly watertight and in as good a state of preservation as on the day it was built. The ground-plan of the oratory is rectangular, 10 ft. 2 in. long, by 15 ft. 3 in. broad, the thickness of the side walls being 4 ft. at the bottom, and that of the end walls 3 ft. 2 in. The two side walls lean inwards, towards each other, with a curved batter, and meet at the top in a straight ridge, covered over with flags 2 ft. wide. The cross section thus resembles a pointed Gothic arch in shape. The end, or gable walls, also have a batter, making the length of the ridge 17 ft., at each end of which was a gable cross, the socket stones of which only remain. The height of the point of the roof is 16 ft. above the ground. The openings consist of a doorway at the west end, with a flat lintel and sloping jambs, 5 ft. 7 in. high, 1 ft. 10 in. wide at the top, and 2 ft. 4 in. wide at the bottom; and a small, round-headed window at the east end, 1 ft. 4 in. high by 10 in. wide outside, splayed towards the inside.

There are two projecting stones, one at each side of the lintel of the doorway within, with holes for the pivots of the door hinges to turn in. Sticking out from the wall inside are three or four stone pegs, similar to those noticed in the bee-hive cells on Skellig Mhichel.

At Kilmalkedar, a mile further north from Gallerus, is another stone roofed dry-built oratory of very similiar construction to the one just described, but in far less perfect condition; and at Tempul Manchain, two miles to the southward, are the remains of another, the west wall and doorway only being left standing.

The class of building, of which the Oratory of Gallerús is the type, was further developed by making the gable walls and the lower part of the side walls vertical instead of sloping, and the surface of the roof flat instead of curved. As examples of this we have St. Macdara's Church, on Macdara's Island, off the coast of Galway, and St. Molaise's Church on Inismurray.[1]

In later times when the size of the churches was increased, it was found that either the stone roof, which was the most suitable kind of covering for a damp climate, would have to be discarded altogether, or some new method of construction would have to be devised, by means of which it might be made to span a wider space without great waste of material. The artifice adopted by the Irish builders in order to get over the difficulty was most ingenious and solved the problem effectually. The church was made in two chambers, one above the other; the lower one being covered with a barrel vault, formed by a semi-circular arch springing from the top of side walls, and the upper one occupying the triangular space between the top of the barrel vault and the under-side of the pointed stone roof of the building on the exterior. The lower chamber was used as the nave, or chancel of the church, and the

[1] For description of stone-roofed oratories in Scotland on the islands of Inchcolm, N. Rona, the Sule Skerry, and at Gallon Head on the I. of Lewis, see T. S. Muir's "Ecclesiological Notes."

upper one, called a croft, may have served as a sleeping apartment for the priest. It was approached by a hole in the barrel vault.

The illustration of St. Macdara's Church in Petrie's "Ecclesiastical Architecture of Ireland" (p. 190), shows very clearly the weakness of a roof composed of stones laid in horizontal courses when the side walls are made too thin and there is no arch to support it beneath. The greater part of this roof has fallen in owing to its structural imperfections. The chancel of St. Molua's Church on Friar's Island, in the Shannon, below Killaloe, has a stone roof laid in horizontal courses, but the walls are thick and the span small. There is also a chamber, 2 ft. high by 1 ft. 3 in. wide, in the top of the roof to reduce the weight of the masonry, in which we have the germ of the croft in the double-chambered churches like St. Kevin's Kitchen, at Glendalough, co. Wicklow. It thus appears that the croft owes its origin to the constructional difficulties encountered in endeavouring to solve the problem of making a stone roof of large span, with a high pitch on the outside to throw off the wet in a damp climate.

The croft was, in the first instance, as at St. Flannan's, Killaloe, merely a space left to lighten the weight of a stone roof entirely laid in flat courses. At St. Kevin's, Glendalough, the principle of the arch is introduced in the barrel-vault used to support the roof, and the croft becomes an upper chamber almost high enough to stand up in. Lastly, at Cormac's Chapel, on the Rock of Cashel, co. Tipperary, both the upper and lower chambers are covered by arched vaulting, the cross section of the former being pointed, and that of the latter semi-circular. The height of the croft is 20 ft., almost equal to that of the chamber below. The only stones laid in horizontal courses are those on the outside of the roof, showing that the overlapping principle was eventually entirely discarded in favour of the arch, for purposes of construction. St. Kevin's Kitchen, at Glendalough, and other double-chambered buildings of the same class, date from the tenth to the twelfth century, and are only mentioned here in order to trace the evolution of the purely national characteristics of Irish architecture from the dry-built forts and clochauns of the Pagan period up to their highest development at the time of the Norman Conquest in A.D. 1169.

With regard to the double stone roof, Mr. James Fergusson remarks, in his "History of Architecture" (vol. ii. p. 232):—"Had the Irish been allowed to persevere in the elaboration of their own style, they would probably have applied this expedient to the roofing of larger buildings than they ever attempted, and might, in so doing, have avoided the greatest falut of Gothic architecture. Without more experience, it is impossible to pronounce to what extent the method might have been carried with safety, or to say whether the Irish double vault is a better constructive form than the single Romance pointed arch. It was certainly an improvement on the wooden roof of the true Gothic style, and its early abandonment is consequently much to be regretted."

All the structures described in this chapter are of stone, for, although we know that many of the early churches were built of wood, no traces of those of the fifth and sixth centuries are now in existence. Many of the small, single-chambered oratories in Ireland, such as Tempul Benen, on Aran Môr, and Cill Cananach, on the middle island of Aran, had wooden roofs, which appear from the gables still standing to have been of high pitch.

Sepulchral Monuments and Remains.

Fortunately we possess ample information as to the methods of burial employed by the Pagan Celts, chiefly derived from the excavations made by Sir R. Colt Hoare in the barrows of Wiltshire, by Mr. Bateman in those of Derbyshire, and by the Rev. Canon Greenwell in those of Yorkshire. The collections derived from these investigations are now preserved in the museums at Devizes and Sheffield, and in the British Museum. The tumuli of Cornwall have been described by Borlase in his "Nenia Cornubiæ," and those of Dorsetshire by Charles Warne in his "Celtic Tumuli of Dorset"; besides numerous other discoveries in different parts of Great Britain, and recorded in the proceedings of the various archæological societies.[1] The Celts of the later Pagan period most commonly disposed of their dead by cremation, and the burnt ashes of the bones, after being enclosed in a rudely baked urn, ornamented with zig-zag lines and other simple patterns, were deposited

[1] The most important of these is by Mr. J. Thurnam in the "Archæologia," vol. xlii. p. 161, and vol. xliii. p. 285. See also Llewellyn Jewitt's "Grave Mounds and their Contents"; Dr. J. Anderson's "Scotland in Pagan Times," 2nd Series.

in the earth. The mouth of the urn was generally covered with a flat stone, and other stones placed round to protect it from the earth. The place of interment was marked either by a mound of earth, a circle of upright stones, a cromlech (*i.e.*, a large flat cap-stone supported on three or four stone props), or a mênhir (*i.e.*, a single standing stone). Some of the more important tumuli have a regularly constructed stone chamber in the centre for the reception of the burial urn, and a passage giving access to it. Often weapons and personal ornaments were deposited in the grave with the cremated ashes of the deceased.[1] When Christianity was introduced, an entire change took place in the methods of sepulture, the chief points of difference being as follows : (1) the Christians did not burn the bodies, but buried them at full length, generally in a direction lying east and west, in a wooden coffin or cist formed of stones surrounding the body ; (2) no objects were placed in the grave with the dead ; (3) the burials were always in consecrated ground associated with a church ; and (4) the monuments were either marked with a cross or inscribed.

For reasons which will be afterwards brought forward there seems to be little doubt that the art of writing was introduced into the Celtic portions of Great Britain at the same time as the Christian religion. The oldest Celtic sepulchral monuments in

[1] The Pagan inhabitants of Britain did not always burn their dead, nor did they always mark the place of sepulture by an overground monument, so that the description here given only applies to the most usual method of disposing of the deceased.

this country have inscriptions in Ogham letters or debased Latin capitals, and may be divided into three classes: (1) those with Ogham letters only; (2) those with debased Latin capitals only; and (3) those with two inscriptions on the same stone, one in Oghams, and the other in debased Latin capitals. The inscriptions in debased Latin capitals are always in the Latin language, and record the name of the deceased, with the formula HIC JACET. The Ogham inscriptions are in the Celtic language, containing, as a rule, nothing more than the name of the deceased and that of his father, connected by the word MAQI (equivalent to the Scotch Mac and the Welsh Map, meaning the son of). Recently a stone has been discovered at Eglwys Cymmyn, in Carmarthenshire, upon which the Celtic word "INIGINA" (meaning daughter of) occurs. (See "Archæologia Cambrensis," 5th ser., vol. vi. p. 224.) Many of the Irish Ogham inscriptions begin with "ANM," perhaps equivalent to the Latin *anima*; other words are found in the middle of the inscriptions that do not seem to be proper names, but the correct translation of which has yet to be made out. The stones on which these inscriptions occur are rude pillars, showing no trace of artificial dressing, varying from 4 ft. to 9 ft. high, placed upright in the ground over the grave of the dead. The inscriptions are incised, and read in a vertical direction, with a very few exceptions. The reasons for believing these stones to be Christian are as follows: (1) by far the greater number are found in association with churches; (2) several have crosses upon them

Modern Capitals.	Debased Latin Capitals.	Saxon Capitals.	Minuscules.	Modern Capitals.	Debased Latin Capitals.	Saxon Capitals.	Minuscules.
A	A	Ⱥ	α	N	ᴎ	Ᵽ	ɳ
B	B	B	ƀ	O	O	☐	o
C	C	⊑	c	P	P	P	ꝑ
D	D	ꝺ	ꝺ	Q	ꝗ	ꝗ	ꝗ
E	E	E	℮	R	R	R	ꞃ
F	F	F	ꝼ	S	S	ꞅ	ſ
G	Ϛ	ᵹ	ꝫ	T	T	ꞇ	ꞇ
H	H	h	h	V	V	u	u
I	‑	I	ı	W		ꝑ	
L	∟	L	l	X		X	x
M	ᴧ	HH	m	Z		ꝫ	z

(No. 2.) Debased Latin and Hiberno-Saxon Alphabets.

p. 66.

of the earliest known forms, which do not seem to have been added after the inscription was cut; (3) the use of the Latin language proves them to belong to a period during or subsequent to the occupation of Britain by the Romans, and yet the well known prefix D.M. of the Roman Pagan epitaphs is entirely wanting; (4) the names mentioned in the inscriptions are in many cases scriptural, or those known to have been adopted by the Christians, or those of early saints; (5) the formulæ of the inscriptions are often Christian; (6) the calling of the deceased as mentioned in the inscriptions sometimes shows him to have been an officer of the church.

The rude pillar stones with Ogham inscriptions only are found chiefly in the south-west of Ireland in the counties of Kerry, Cork, Waterford, and Kilkenny, and a few in Scotland; those with debased Latin inscriptions in Wales, Cornwall, and Devon; and those with bi-literal inscriptions (in both Oghams and debased Latin capitals) in Pembrokeshire, Carmarthenshire, and Brecknockshire. The exact number of these monuments and their geographical distribution will be seen from the table on pp. 68, 69, prepared from R. R. Brash's "Ogham Inscribed Monuments of the Gaedhil"; Sir S. Ferguson's "Ogham Inscriptions in Ireland, Wales, and Scotland"; Professor I. O. Westwood's "Lapidarium Walliæ"; and Æ. Hübner's "Inscriptiones Britanniæ Christianæ."

The origin of the Ogham alphabet has not yet been satisfactorily arrived at, although ingenious suggestions have been made on the subject by the Rev. Canon Isaac Taylor in his "Greeks and Goths,"

	Oghams only.		Latin Capitals only.		Bi-literal.	
ENGLAND—						
Cornwall ...	—	—	17	17	—	—
Devonsh. ...	—	—	5	5	2	2
Isle of Man ...	3	4	1	1	—	—
WALES—						
Anglesey ...	—	—	6	6	—	—
Brecknocksh....	—	—	5	6	3	3
Cardigansh. ...	—	—	5	5	1	1
Carmarthensh.	1	1	13	14	4	4
Carnarvonsh....	—	—	8	13	—	—
Denbighsh. ...	—	—	2	2	1	1
Flintsh.	—	—	1	1	—	—
Glamorgansh...	1	1	7	7	1	1
Merionethsh....	—	—	4	4	—	—
Montgomerysh.	—	—	1	1	—	—
Pembrokesh. ...	3	4	6	7	7	8
SCOTLAND—						
Aberdeensh. ...	2	2	—	—	1	1
Edinburgsh. ...	—	—	1	1	—	—
Fifesh.	1	1	—	—	—	—
Orkney	1	1	—	—	—	—
Shetland... ...	5	7	—	—	—	—
Selkirksh. ...	—	—	1	1	—	—
Sutherland ...	1	1	—	—	—	—
Wigtonsh. ...	—	—	2	4	—	—
IRELAND—						
Co. Armagh ...	1	1	—	—	—	—
,, Carlow ...	1	1	—	—	—	—
,, Cavan ...	1	1	—	—	—	—
,, Clare ..	1	1	—	—	—	—
,, Cork ...	30	47	—	—	—	—
,, Enniskillen	1	1	—	—	—	—
,, Fermanagh	1	1	—	—	—	—
,, Galway ...	1	1	—	—	—	—
,, Kerry ...	54	77	—	—	—	—
,, Kildare ...	1	3	—	—	—	—
,, Kilkenny...	5	6	—	—	1	1
King's Co. ...	—	—	—	—	1	1
Co. Limerick ...	1	1	—	—	—	—
,, Lond'nderry	1	1	—	—	—	—
,, Mayo... ...	1	1	—	—	—	—
,. Monaghan	1	1	—	—	—	—

	Oghams only		Latin Capitals only.		Bi-literal.	
IRELAND—*continued.*						
Co. Roscommon	1	2	—	—	—	—
,, Tyrone ...	1	1	—	—	—	—
,, Waterford	15	36	—	—	—	—
,, Wexford ...	1	1	—	—	—	—
,, Wicklow ...	2	2	—	—	—	—
	139	208	85	95	22	23

NOTE.—The first column of numbers refers to the localities, and the second to the stones, as in some cases there is more than one stone in each locality.

and by Prof. John Rhys in his " Lectures on Welsh Philology."

As Ogham inscriptions are not found outside Great Britain, and are most numerous in the south-west of Ireland and South Wales, it appears to be probable that this form of letter was invented either in Pembrokeshire or Kerry. There are certain resemblances between the Ogham and the Runic alphabets, both having letters made with straight strokes, branching out of a stem line, and both being divided up into groups or classes of letters; but it has not yet been proved that one was derived from the other. The Ogham alphabet is called the " Bethluisnion," from the names of the first, second, and last letters of the first group. It consists of twenty letters divided into four groups of five each. The letters are formed of straight strokes branching out from a stem line, or else drawn right across it.[1]

The requisite number of variations are obtained

[1] The stem line is called " Druim," or ridge, and the cross strokes " Fleasg," or twig.

by altering the number of the cross strokes, by altering the side of the line on which they occur, and by altering the direction in which they cut the stem line.

We thus get five groups as follows :—

The B " aicme " (or kind).

Strokes numbering from 1 to 5, drawn at right angles to the stem line below.

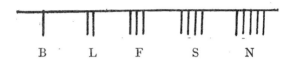

B L F S N

The H " aicme."

Strokes numbering from 1 to 5, drawn at right angles to the stem line above.

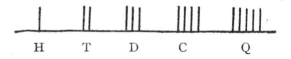

H T D C Q

The M " aicme."

Long strokes numbering from 1 to 5, cutting the stem line diagonally.

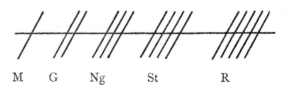

M G Ng St R

(No. 3.)
Pillar-stone of Severus at Nanscow, with Inscription in Debased
Latin Capitals.
(From a drawing by ARTHUR G. LANGDON.)
Scale $\frac{1}{12}$ real size.

The A "aicme."

Short strokes numbering from 1 to 5, cutting the stem line at right angles.

The names of the letters are taken from those of trees as follows :—

	B	Beith	Birch
	L	Luis	Quicken
	F	Fearn	Alder
	S	Sail	Sallow
	N	Nion	Ash

	H	Huath	Hawthorn
	D	Duir	Oak
	T	Tinne	Holly
	C	Coll	Hazle
	Q	Queirt	Apple

	M	Muin	Vine
	G	Gort	Ivy
	Ng	Ngedal	Reed
	St	Straif	Blackthorn
	R	Ruis	Elder.

A	Ailm	Fir
O	Orm	Furze
U	Ur	Heath
E	Eadhadh	Aspen
I	Ihadh	Yew

There are in addition five other letters called "forfeada," or "over trees," only the first[1] and second[2] of which occur on lapidary inscriptions :—

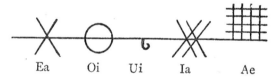

Ea   Oi   Ui   Ia   Ae

Most of the Ogham inscriptions read from left to right when the stem line is placed horizontally, or from the bottom upwards when it is placed vertically; but there are exceptions, as in the case of the stone from Montaggart, co. Cork, now in the Museum of the Royal Irish Academy.[3] One of the greatest drawbacks to the study of Ogham inscriptions is the uncertainty of the readings arising

---

[1] At Crickhowell in Brecknockshire and several places in Ireland.

[2] At Bressay in Shetland.

[3] Brash's "Ogham Monuments," p. 162; Sir S. Ferguson's "Ogham Inscriptions," p. 89.

from the following causes :—(1) Doubt as to whether the whole should be read backwards or forwards, *i.e.*, from left to right or from right to left ; (2) doubt as to whether the inscription is placed in the proper position to be read, *i.e.*, with a particular set of strokes representing a letter on the upper or the under side of the line ; (3) inexact spacing of the strokes forming the letters or of the words ; (4) weathering of the strokes at the end or beginning of a letter or on one side of the stem line ; and (5) irregularity in the stem line itself.

The uncertainty as to the direction in which the inscription should be read and as to the position in which it should be placed gives rise to four different readings. Thus the first group placed in its proper position reads from left to right BLFSN, and from right to left NSFLB ; but if turned upside down and read from left to right it becomes QCTDH (or the second group read backwards), and if from right to left HDTCQ. In most of the Ogham lapidary inscriptions found in Ireland and Wales the angle of the stone is made to serve as a stem line, the letters being cut on two different faces ; but on some of the Scotch examples there is a regular stem line in the middle of one face, and the words are separated by double dots.

The discovery of the first Ogham stone in Ireland is due to Edward Lhuyd, the father of Welsh archæology, who copied the inscription on a pillar at Trabeg, near Dingle, co. Kerry, as early as the year 1707. In 1784 the stone at Mount Callan, co. Clare, was noticed by T. O'Flanagan ; in 1790 H. Pelham,

Lord Lansdowne's agent in the co. Kerry, found twelve more, which were published in 1796 in the eighth vol. of General Vallancey's "Collectanea de Rebus Hibernicis," together with the Ogham alphabet from the Book of Ballymote. In the present century J. Windele found about twenty-eight more Ogham inscriptions in the counties of Cork, Waterford, and Kerry between 1830 and 1838, but no serious attempt was made to explain their meaning until the Right Rev. Dr. Charles Graves, Bishop of Limerick, read a paper before the Royal Irish Academy in 1848, "On a general method of deciphering secret alphabetic writings."[1] Since this time our knowledge of the subject has been considerably increased by the labours of Sir S. Ferguson, R. Rolt Brash, Professor I. O. Westwood, and Professor John Rhys.

The key to the Ogham alphabet is given in the Book of Ballymote, a MS. in the library of the Royal Irish Academy, compiled A.D. 1370-1390, and has never been lost among the common people by whom it is preserved in a doggerel rhyme beginning—

> "For B one stroke at your right hand,
> And L doth always two demand ;
> For F draw three ; for S make four ;
> When you want N you add one more."

Sir S. Ferguson[2] quotes an instance of a man, named Collins, living in the co. Cork, who was in

---

[1] R. Hitchcock was employed by Dr. Graves in 1845 to collect inscriptions for this paper and discovered several new examples.

[2] "Ogham Inscriptions," p. 12.

recent times summoned before the magistrates for putting his name on his cart in Ogham letters.

The Right Rev. Bishop Graves proved the accuracy of the key handed down traditionally, and found in the MSS. by applying the cipher test. This consists in getting together a sufficiently large number of inscriptions and classifying the letters in them according to the frequency with which they occur. Then, assuming the language to be Irish, the sounds, or the letters which represent them, in several pages of an ancient MS. are treated in the same way. It follows that the letter of unknown meaning in the cipher that occurs most often must correspond with the letter or sound of known meaning that occurs most often in the pages of the MSS. and so on with the rest.[1] Dr. Graves also pointed out the significance of the group of letters forming the word MAQI, the old form of MAC, or son of, the very common occurrence of which had been already noticed by the Rev. M. Horgan.

Further confirmation of the accuracy of the key to the Ogham alphabet has since been obtained from the bi-literal and bi-lingual inscriptions, of which the most interesting is that at St. Dogmael's in Pembrokeshire. The inscription in debased Latin capitals reads :—

SAGRAMNI FILI CUNOTAMI,

and the Oghams correspond almost exactly—

SAGRANI MAQI CUNATAMI.

---

[1] The method of discovering the meaning of a cipher is well explained in Edgar Allan's Poe's tale of the Golden Beetle.

Quite recently an equally perfect bi-literal inscription has been discovered at Eglwys Cymmyn, in Carmarthenshire. The Latin inscription reads :—

AVITORIA FILIA CVNIGNI,

and the Oghams—

AVITTORIGES INIGINA CVNIGNI.

The origin of the Ogham alphabet is ascribed in the "Book of Ballymote," to Ogma, one of the learned men of the mythical Tuatha de Danan race, and in a MS. in the British Museum (Add. 4783), Breas mac Elathan is said to have been the inventor. Oghams are continually referred to in the Irish MSS., such as the Books of Leinster, Ballymote, Lismore, and the Leabhar na Uidre, generally as being carved on sepulchral monuments, but sometimes on objects of metal. The inscriptions on the Ogham pillars, and the nature of localities in which they are found, prove conclusively that they were originally erected to commemorate the dead. The point we have now to determine is how far they are Christian.

Two of the authorities who have written on the subject come to diametrically opposite conclusions. Sir S. Ferguson, says,[1] "I shall be able, however, I think, to show reasonable grounds for believing that the bulk, if not all, of our Ogham monuments are Christian ; that some of them represent, perhaps, as old a Christianity as has ever been claimed for the Church in either island ; and that the 'Scoti in Christo credentes,' to whom Palladius was sent by

---

[1] " Ogham Inscriptions," p. 18.

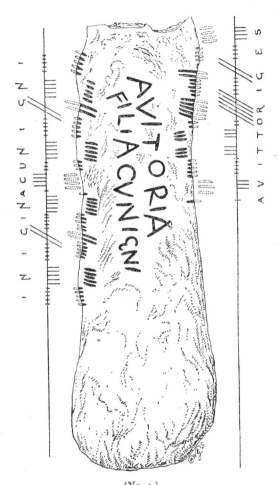

(No. 4.)
Pillar-stone of Avitoria, at Eglwys Cymmyn, with bi-literal inscriptions in Debased Latin Capitals and in Oghams.
(From a drawing by WORTHINGTON G. SMITH.)
Scale ⅛ real size.

p. 76.

Pope Celestine in the fifth century, a more numerous and better organised community than has generally been supposed." Mr. R. Rolt Brash [1] believes that the Ogham alphabet is of Pagan origin, and that most of the stones inscribed with this form of letter belong to the pre-Christian period.

Out of the Ogham inscribed stones now existing in Ireland, fifty-two have been found in underground chambers inside raths, forty-nine in ancient burial-grounds called "killeens," and twenty-nine in churches or churchyards.

Mr. R. Rolt Brash describes the general appearance of a "killeen" [2] in his " Ogham inscribed monuments of the Gaedhil," as being a circular area, slightly raised above the level of the surrounding land, and generally enclosed with a low rampart of earth, or sometimes a circle of upright stones. "Killeens" are not usually near any church, and at the present day are only used for burying unbaptized infants and suicides. The ancient interments consist of uncremated bodies surrounded by stones set on edge so as to form a cist. Mr. Rolt Brash unhesitatingly assigns the "killeens" to the Pagan period, but the fact that they still retain what Sir S. Ferguson calls "a semi-sacred, yet not quite holy character," and that superstitious ceremonies [3] continue to be performed within

[1] "Inscribed Monuments of the Gaedhil."

[2] There are several different forms of this word, "keel," "killeena " and " kealuragh."

[3] Mr. Brash notes several instances in killeens where there are Ogham monuments, at Knockrour, Shancloon, and Kilcaskan, co. Cork, and at Drumloghan, co. Waterford. The ceremony consists in saying certain prayers, whilst making the

their precincts seems to point to a Christian origin. The Ogham inscribed stones occur in groups within some of the "killeens," instead of singly, as in the county Kerry at Ballintaggart, where there are as many as nine, at Ballinrannig seven, and Kilcolaght six, also in the county Waterford, at Kilgravane five. In the case of the stones found in the rath caves, the same thing is observable, there being ten at Drumloghan, county Waterford, seven at Dunloe, county Kerry, six at Ballyhank, three at Aghaliskey, and three at Roovesmore, county Cork. Since the rath caves are generally in close proximity to "killeens," the inference seems to be that the builders of the caves obtained their materials from the neighbouring burial grounds, which are therefore of earlier date. Almost every rath or circular earthwork in Ireland has within its area one or more underground chambers connected by passages, resembling in construction the "eirde houses" of Scotland, and the artificial caves of Cornwall. The side walls of these crypts are either built entirely of rubble masonry without cement, or formed of upright pillars filled in between with smaller stones, the whole being roofed over with flat slabs, and covered with earth. The generally received opinion seems to be that these souterrains were used as storehouses in times of peace, and as places of secure retreat when any danger threatened. Some of them are provided with

circuit of the killeen sunwise, and dropping votive offerings into a rude stone basin called a "bullaun," or hanging pieces of rag on the thorn bushes (see R. Brash's "Ogham Inscribed Monuments of the Graedhil," pp. 133, 153, 167 and 273).

an ingenious sort of trap-door entrance to the inner chambers to make access more difficult in case of sudden attack from without. Pieces of Samian ware have been discovered in the "eirde houses" of Scotland, indicating that they were in use during the period of the Roman occupation or soon after, and the souterrains in Ireland are possibly of the same age.

None of the Ogham inscribed stones from the rath caves bear any Christian symbol, but, in the underground structure at Aghacarrible, co. Kerry, where two Ogham pillars are built into the side walls of the chamber, incised crosses are carved on one of the adjoining stones. There are in Ireland twenty-three Ogham monuments with crosses upon them, six of which occur in killeens, and eight in churchyards; the remainder not being near any building either Christian or Pagan. Mr. Rolt Brash assumes that the crosses have been, in all cases, cut a long time after the inscription, but there is no sufficient evidence to show that this is so. The crosses are invariably of early form, either a plain Latin cross or a Maltese cross within a circle, and incised, instead of being carved in relief. The finest specimens are at Aglish, Brandon Mountain, Ballymorereigh, Maumenorigh, and Trabeg, all in the co. Kerry; and at Drumconwell, co. Armagh.

Ogham inscribed stones are often found associated with oratories bearing the names of early saints, as at Tempulleen Fachtna, co. Cork; St. Brendan's Cell on Inisvicillane (Blasket Islands); Kilfountain, Kilmalkedar, and Temple Manahan, co. Kerry; and

St. Declan's, Ardmore, co. Waterford   At Agha-
bulloge, co. Cork, is an Ogham pillar associated
traditionally with St. Olan, surmounted by an oval
cap-stone, supposed to possess miraculous properties.
In Scotland there are twelve Ogham inscriptions,
out of which six are on slabs bearing sculptured
crosses, in most cases covered with interlaced work,
and accompanied by the curious symbols which
occur so frequently in this part of Great Britain.

One of these stones was found in the Pictish
tower at Burrian in Orkney, but most of the others
are now, or were originally, in churchyards.   The
character of the inscriptions resembles that of the
scholastic Oghams of the MSS., with divisions between
the words and the stem line, so that it is probable
that the Scotch Oghams are of later date than those
of Ireland and Wales.   The greater part of them are
undoubtedly Christian, for there is no question here
as to the possibility of the crosses having been added
after the inscriptions, as the disposition of the ornamental features shows that this could not have been
the case.

In Wales there are twenty-four Ogham monuments,
six of which bear incised crosses, either of the plain
Latin form, or surrounded by a circle.   With only six
exceptions the inscriptions are bi-literal and bi-lingual,
one epitaph being in Oghams and in the Celtic
language, and the other in debased Latin capitals
and in the Latin tongue.   Almost all the stones are
found in association with churches, and are therefore
presumably Christian; but, at Loughor, in Glamorganshire, there is a Roman altar with Oghams

cut on the edge, which may possibly belong to the
Pagan period.

The existence of the bi-literal inscriptions shows
that the Ogham character was in use at the same time
as the Latin letters ; but there are a great number of
rude pillar stones in Wales, Cornwall, and Scotland,
with inscriptions in Latin letters only. It has not
yet been decided whether the Britons learnt the use
of letters from the Romans, or whether the art of
writing was introduced with Christianity by the first
missionaries ; but, however this may be, the oldest
inscriptions, except the Oghams, are rude copies of
the Roman alphabet, most of the letters being in the
capital form. The chief peculiarities are that the
size and shape of the letters are not uniform, that the
letters are sometimes placed upside down, backwards,
or sideways, and that two letters are run together,
as in the Roman inscriptions. The smaller letters, or
minuscules, were not introduced until about the sixth
century, so that, when they are found mixed with the
capitals, it is an indication of late date. Most of the
rude pillar stones with debased Latin inscriptions
are found in churchyards, and a large number can
be proved to be Christian by crosses cut upon the
stones, by the formulæ of the inscriptions, and by
the names mentioned in them. Some of these
monuments, although not now connected with any
church, mark the site of an ancient Christian
burial place. Thus, "in making the Holyhead
railway between Lima and Cernioge (Denbighshire),
whilst cutting through a field called Doltrebeddw,
about forty graves were discovered, most of them

about two yards long, cased with rough stones, and lying within a compass of 20 yards by 10. Bones were found in most of them, but not the least vestige of coffins. On the underside of one stone, which covered one of the most perfect of the graves, was found an inscription in rude Roman characters with several of the letters conjoined, which reads

BROHOMAGLI IAM IC JACET
ET VXOR EIVS CAVNE."[1]

A similar discovery of graves was made near the Cat-stane, not far from Edinburgh.

The symbols on the rude pillar stones with inscriptions consist of the Chi-Rho monogram and the cross. Examples of the former exist at St. Just, in Penwith, in Cornwall, at Penmachno, in Caernarvonshire, and at Kirkmadrine and Whithorn, in Wigtownshire. Crosses of early form also are to be found on stones at Margam Mountain, in Glamorganshire, at St. Clement's, Truro, and Castledôr, in Cornwall. It will not be necessary to describe the whole of these, as a specimen of each class will be sufficient. In the old church-yard at Kirkmadrine, on the most southerly promontory of Wigtownshire, there were at one time three inscribed stones marked with the Chi-Rho monogram, but one has now disappeared. The largest of the two now remaining is a block of whinstone, 5 ft. high and 1 ft 6 in. broad, having the Christian monogram within a circle surmounted

[1] I. O. Westwood's " Lapidarium Walliæ," p. 202.

by the Alpha and Omega, and with the following
inscription in debased Latin capitals below :—

HIC IACENT SCI ET PRAECIPVI
SACERDOTES VIVENTIVS ET MAVORIVS.

(Here lie the holy and excellent priests, Viventius
and Mavorius.)

The use of the monogram in Rome began in the
time of Constantine (A.D. 312), and in Gaul it is
found on dated inscriptions between (A.D. 377 to
493). On the opposite side of Glenluce Bay to
Kirkmadrine is Whithorn, the "Ad Candidam
Casam," where Bede tells us that St. Ninian built his
first stone church, and dedicated it to St. Martin of
Tours, when he came to convert the Southern Picts.
There is also at Whithorn an inscribed stone with the
monogram carved upon it, and there is no reason why
this, as well as the ones at Kirkmadrine should not
be of the time of St. Ninian's mission (A.D. 410 to
432).

The pillar on Margam Mountain in Glamorganshire, is 5 ft. high, 1 ft. 6 ins. wide, by 1 ft. thick,
having an incised cross of the Maltese form on the
top, and the following inscription in debased Latin
capitals on the face :—

BODVOCI HIC IACIT FILIVS CATOTIGIRNI
PRONEPVS ETERNALI VEDOMAVI.

The names, formulæ, and other peculiarities of
the debased Latin inscriptions in Great Britain are
all carefully tabulated by Æmilius Hübner in his
"Inscriptiones Britanniæ Christianæ." The most

common formula is HIC IACET, sometimes with
the addition IN HOC TVMVLO or IN HOC
CONGERIES LAPIDVM. Although the formula
HIC IACET occurs on epitaphs in the Catacombs
at Rome, it is not distinctively Christian, but in three
instances IN PACE is found, namely, at Llanerfyl, in
Montgomeryshire, at Llansadwrn, in Anglesey, and at
Hayle, in Cornwall. The inscription on the pillar
stone at Bedd Porius, in Merionethshire, is supposed
to read :—

PORIVS HIC IN TVMVLO IACIT HOMO
XPIANVS FVIT.

(Porius lies buried in this mound.　He was a
Christian.)

Some of the stones with debased Latin inscriptions
are associated with the names of early British saints.
At Dolaucothy House, in Caermarthenshire, is preserved the tombstone of St. Paulinus, which came
from Pant-y-Polion, inscribed in debased Latin
capitals : " Servator fidei, patriæque semper amator
Hic Paulinus jacet, cultor pientissimus æqui." This
Saint is mentioned in the lives of St. David and St.
Teilo, as having taught St. David to read, and as
having been present at the Synod of Llandewi Brefi
(A.D. 519). He was one of the numerous learned
men who are connected with the College founded by
St. Iltutus, at Llantwit Major, in Glamorganshire.
At Llansadwrn, in Anglesea, is the tombstone of the
patron saint, Sadwrn Farchog, the brother of St.
Iltutus, who accompanied Cadfan to Britain in his
old age. It is inscribed : " Hic beatus Saturninus

se (pultus) (i) acit et sua sa (ncta) conjux pa (ce)."
(Here lies buried St. Sadwrn and his holy wife in
peace.)

In a field near the church of Llangan in Caermarthenshire, and near a holy well called Ffynnon
Canna, is the stone chair of the patron saint with
her name CANNA inscribed in debased Latin
capitals upon it. St. Canna was cousin and sister-
in-law of St. Iltutus, and the church at Llangan, in
Glamorganshire, is also dedicated to her.

Sometimes the inscriptions on the rude pillar
stones give the office of the deceased by which the
Christian origin is clearly demonstrated, as on the
sepulchral monuments of Senachus and Meracius
at Cefn Amlwch, in Caernarvonshire, who are desig-
nated $\overline{\text{PRB}}$ or bishops, and that of the priests
Viventius and Mavorius at Kirkmadrine, already
described.

It is not to be supposed that the gravestones of
the early Celtic Christians were always inscribed, for
probably the ordinary form of memorial erected to
the deceased was simply marked with an incised
cross. It is, however, very difficult in the absence
of an inscription or ornamental features to determine
the age of a tombstone bearing a cross only, but
probably when found in association with the oldest
type of dry-built church, as on Skelig Mhichel,
co. Kerry, and on Eilean-na-Naoimh, Garveloch
Islands, the structures and the surrounding monuments are of the same date. Rude pillar stones
with inscriptions are sometimes found side by side
with those having an incised cross, but no lettering,

as at Traws-mawr, in Caermarthenshire, and the inference is here also that both were erected at the same period.

We have now endeavoured to acquaint the reader with such facts as will enable him to form some idea of the general appearance of the primitive Celtic churches and their surroundings. The chief characteristics of the buildings are that they are constructed after the Pagan fashion existing in Ireland at the time of the introduction of Christianity ; that there is an entire absence of either ornamental or architectural features, such as mouldings and sculpture; that the ground-plan is of the simplest possible kind and of very small size ; that the dwellings of the monks are grouped round the church; and that the whole is enclosed within a stone wall, which was in the first instance defensive, but afterwards used for the sake of seclusion. The sepulchral monuments, like the buildings, are completely devoid of ornament or tooling,[1] and consist generally of a rude pillar stone, marked with the Chi Rho monogram on the plainest form of cross,

---

[1] The Ogham inscribed stone from Llywell, in Brecknockshire, now in the British Museum, is an exception to this rule, one face being covered with the rudest possible attempts at ornament, amongst which appears to be an ecclesiastic holding a crozier. The only other instance of sculpture on a monument of this kind, that has come under my notice, is a bust of our Lord incised on the pillar forming one of the gate-posts at the entrance of the cemetery of Killeen Cormac, co. Kildare, the opposite pillar bearing the well-known IVVERE DRVIDES inscription. (See " Proc. Royal Irish Academy,"—" Antiquities," vol. ix, p. 253.)

sometimes accompanied by an inscription in Oghams, or debased Latin capitals.

The portable objects which belonged to the church at this early period are now no longer in existence, unless the iron bell of St. Patrick is really a relic of that saint, as it professes to be.

The subject of the Celtic portable bells will be considered in a future chapter, so that it will not be necessary to refer to it further in this place.

CHAPTER III.

THE ARCHÆOLOGY OF THE POST-AUGUSTINIAN OR LATER CELTIC CHURCH (A.D. 600–1066).

Structures.

IT has been found convenient to divide the architecture of the Celtic church into two periods, the division being drawn at the time of the landing of St. Augustine in Kent at the end of the sixth century, but it is not to be supposed that the changes in style took place suddenly. The effect produced by the conversion of the Saxons from Paganism was to remove the barrier which had shut out Ireland from intercourse with the rest of Europe during the fifth and sixth centuries, and thus gradually to assimilate the character of the ecclesiastical buildings to that existing in other parts of Christendom.

It has been shown in a previous chapter that the typical church of the early Celtic period was of small size, simple in ground-plan, with only one door and one window, and entirely devoid of architectural or ornamental features of any description. The most important changes which took place subsequently were the extension of the ground-plan by the addition of the chancel and the bell-tower ; the improvement of the methods of construction by the introduction of the principle of the arch and the use of cement; and the embellishment of the whole by the employment of mouldings and figure sculpture. These developments were the direct result of Continental influence upon the architecture of Ireland, which, although it preserved enough of the features derived from the Pagan-Celtic modes of building to give it an individuality of its own, was nevertheless in its later phases merely a special variety of the Romanesque style found in other parts of Europe.

It is impossible, therefore, to understand the meaning of many of the peculiarities of Irish architecture without some knowledge of the different foreign styles which existed at the same period, and there is no book that gives a better account of the relations between them than Dr. E. A. Freeman's "History of Architecture." The first churches in Italy before about A.D. 400 were copied from the Roman basilica, and all the details were Classical, but, when the seat of government was removed to Constantinople, Eastern influence began to make itself felt, producing the Byzantine style; and, lastly, the introduction of the Northern Teutonic element at the time of the Lombard invasion in A.D. 568 resulted in the creation of the Romanesque style. The principal feature of Byzantine architecture is the dome; and St. Sophia at Constantinople, or St. Vitale at Ravenna, may be taken as typical specimens. The Romanesque style is so called because it is partly an imitation of Roman, but, as Dr. Freeman [1] tells us, the Lombards "inspired new life into the dying embers, and added harmony to the yet disjointed parts; Basilican and

[1] "Hist. of Architecture," p. 177.

Byzantine architecture each contributed its choicest beauties to form a style, which in Italy itself produced far from despicable fruits, and gave birth to a yet more glorious offspring in the wondrous churches of Rhenish Germany. The chief characteristics of Lombard architecture are the new forms given to the pillars, and their more extended application as decorative features ; a new style of sculpture ; a more extended use of vaulting ; an entirely new ground-plan and outline of churches ; and, finally, by no means the least important innovation, the introduction of steeples or belfries." Dr. Freeman [1] also, in describing the so-called palace of Theodoric at Ravenna, which is attributed by Mr. Hope to the Lombard kings, observes :—" In this first of Teutonic buildings, every mind not quite warped by the pedantry of Classicalism must at once recognise not only a wonderful change but a wonderful improvement. The architect at once grasped the great law that the construction and decoration must be derived from the same source. The chief constructive principle of Roman architecture is the round arch ; here it becomes for the first time the great source of decoration. We have here no ancient or modern Italian mock façade, with useless colonnades, unmeaning entablatures, and sham pediments, but a front which at first sight might be the work of Gundulph or Walkelyn."

Dr. Freeman, in another place, defines Roman [2] architecture as a "futile attempt to combine the arch and the entablature." "It is," he says, "a transition from Grecian to Romanesque, from the consistent system of the entablature to the consistent system of the round arch. It strives to engraft its own system of construction upon that of Greece, the latter being consequently reduced to a mere source of adventitious decoration. The decorative, merely decorative, entablature is thrust prominently forward, and the arch, the real construction, is obscured, and thrust as far as possible out of sight." It was only in engineering structures, such as their great aqueducts, that the Romans ventured to use the arch boldly, without any attempt at concealment.

In the earliest buildings existing in Ireland the roofs are composed of stones laid in horizontal courses, overlapping each other until they meet at the top, and all the openings are spanned by a flat lintel. The style is, therefore, that of the entablature, and the introduction of the principle of the arch produced as marked a change in the character of the churches of Ireland as took place in Italy when the Lombards finally discarded the traditions of Classical art and invented the Romanesque style. The change from the entablature to the arch was not, however, a sudden one, for the flat lintel survived in the doorways long after the opening between the nave and the chancel was spanned by a semi-circular arch. In the earlier single-chamber churches, with small doors and windows, the arch was superfluous, but when a second chamber was added, and the size of the opening between the nave and chancel was increased, the arch became a necessity. There are two classes of churches in Ireland, one in which the capacity was enlarged by adding a second chamber, and the other by making the dimensions of the single chamber greater. The early oratories varied in size from 9 ft. to 19 ft. long by 6 ft. to 11 ft. wide, as will be seen from the following table :—

	ft.	in.		ft.	in.
Skelig Mhichel	... 10	0	by	6	0
Oilen Tsenach...	... 14	0	,,	9	0
Ardoilean	... 14	0	,,	10	0
St. Brendan's, Inisglora ...	... 12	0	,,	8	6
Kilmalkedar, co. Kerry ...	... 17	0	,,	10	0
Gallarus, co. Kerry	... 15	3	,,	10	2
St. Molaga's, co. Cork ...	... 13	0	,,	9	8
St. Declan's, Ardmore ...	... 13	4	,,	8	9
St. Molaise's, Innismury ...	... 8	10	,,	7	10
St. Mac Dara's	... 15	0	,,	11	0
St. Bennen's, Aran	... 10	9	,,	7	0
Cill Cannanach, Aran ...	... 13	0	,,	8	6
St. Enda's, Aran	... 19	6	,,	9	8
St. Gobnet's, Aran	... 12	8	,,	8	6
Tempull Sula-Sgeir, Western Islands	14	0	,,	8	0
Tigh Beannachadh, Gallon Head ...	18	2	,,	10	4

In later times dimensions were increased as in the following examples :—

	ft.	in.		ft.	in.
St. Cronan's, co. Clare ...	... 22	0	by	13	0
St. Martin's, co. Kerry ...	... 32	8	,,	12	10
Dulane, co. Meath	... 35	0	,,	21	0
St. Dervila's, co. Mayo ...	... 42	0	,,	17	6
Maghera, co. Londonderry ...	... 71	10	,,	20	5

It appears, then, that the primitive oratories can be distinguished from the later single-chamber churches by the size of the ground-plan, as the length of the former never exceeded 20 ft. or the breadth 11 ft. interior dimensions. This smallness of size may, to a certain extent, be accounted for by the difficulty that would be experienced in roofing over a wide span without a knowledge either of the principle of the arch in constructing a vaulted covering, or such skill in carpentry as would be required to design a large trussed roof of wood.

The old Irish builders seem to have excelled more in the art of masonry than in carpentry, and they adhered to the national stone roof to the very last, partly because it had been handed down to them from their forefathers, and partly because it was the best possible kind of covering in a damp climate. The limitations thus placed upon the size of the churches in Ireland led to the practice of erecting several in one place, the later ones generally being of slightly increased dimensions. As instances of this there are groups of three churches on Inniscaltra, co. Clare, and at Kilmacduagh, co. Clare; four on Scattery Island, co. Clare; and seven at Clonmacnois, King's County; and at Glendalough, co. Wicklow.

The double-chambered churches were sometimes formed out of a single-chambered building, by the addition of a nave at the west end, as seems to have been the case at St. Molua's, on Friar's Island, near Killaloe, co. Clare, where the chancel is the original stone-roofed oratory of St. Molua. When an alteration of this kind was made the western doorway was enlarged for the insertion of a chancel arch. In the earliest type of double-chambered church the opening between the nave and chancel was very narrow.

The two best specimens of churches showing the transition between the single and the double-chambered type are not in Ireland but in Scotland.[1] One is at Lybster, in Reay, Caithness, consisting of a nave 18 ft. long by 11 ft. wide, and a chancel 9 ft. square interior dimensions. The west doorway is of the same shape and size as the opening between the nave and chancel, both being flat-headed, and both having inclining jambs like those in Ireland. The other is at Weir, in Orkney, consisting of a nave 19 ft. 2 in. long by 12 ft. 10 in. wide, and a chancel 7 ft. 10 in. long by 7 ft. 2 in. wide interior dimensions. The west doorway and the opening between the nave and chancel are of the same size and shape, 2 ft. 6 in. wide, and having a rude semi-circular arch of thin, slaty stone at the top. With regard to these two buildings, Dr. J. Anderson[2] remarks :—"The chancel arch is the characteristic feature of all churches of this typical form. Its character indicates the character of the building, and marks the advancement of style. And though we cannot say of the round chancel arch at Weir, or the flat-headed substitute for a chancel arch at Lybster, that they are the earliest specimens extant, we can say that no earlier type of chancel entrance is likely to be found than one which, whether it be round-headed like Weir, or flat-headed like Lybster, it is not differentiated in any feature of size, construction, form, or ornament from the external doorway."

[1] See T. S. Muir's "Ecclesiological Notes on some of the Islands of Scotland," pp. 108 and 114.

[2] "Scotland in Early Christian Times," 1st series, p. 63.

There are a few instances in Saxon architecture in England where the chancel arches do not differ from the doorways as regards size and shape, as at Bradford-on-Avon, Wilts, where the chancel arch is only 3 ft. 5 in. wide; but in Ireland, if such transitional features ever existed, they have now entirely disappeared. One of the earliest typical specimens of a church consisting of a nave and chancel in Ireland is that dedicated to the Trinity, at Glendalough, co. Wicklow. The nave is 29 ft. 6 in. long by 17 ft. 6 in. wide, and the chancel 13 ft. 6 in. long by 9 ft. wide, interior dimensions, the walls being 2 ft. 6 in. thick. The chancel arch is semi-circular, built of neatly-dressed granite stones on each face, filled in with slate rubble between, and entirely devoid of mouldings or impost to spring from. The span is the full width of the chancel, 9 ft. The openings in the walls of the nave consist of a western doorway, with flat lintel and inclining jambs, 6 ft. 2 in. high, 2 ft. 5 in. wide at the top, and 2 ft. 7 in. wide at the bottom ; and a south window.

The chancel has a round-headed east window, with inclining jambs, 2 ft. 6 in. high, 10 in. wide at the top and 1 ft. wide at the bottom ; and a triangular-headed south window, 1 ft. 7 in. high by 8 in. wide. There are no mouldings in any part of the church, and the only architectural features are, a flat slab projecting 2 in. from the wall above the east window of the chancel, and two stone brackets, sticking out at right angles to the east wall of the chancel at the bottom of the gable of the roof. These curious gargoyle-like projections are peculiar to Irish ecclesiastical buildings, and they seem to be intended simply for ornament, as there is no apparent use to which they could be put, unless the roof was carried beyond the gable walls and the bracket was used to support a barge-board.[1]   In the earliest churches, as at Cill Cananach, in the Middle Island of Aran, these projecting stones are rectangular and are not dressed at all; but in the late examples at Oughtmama and Tempul Chronain, co. Clare, they are cut away on the under-side, so that the stone gets thinner towards its extreme end.   Somewhat similar corbels are to be seen in English buildings forming a finish to the coping of the gable of the roof, but projecting at right angles to the walls from which the roof springs, not, as in Ireland, at right angles to the gable walls.

Another remarkable feature in Irish architecture is the way in which the side walls are prolonged, so as to form pilasters projecting from the end walls. When the roof was of stone, as in the case of the church on St. Mac Dara's Island, off the west coast of Galway, the pilaster was carried right round the gable, but generally it stopped at the level of the springing of the roof, as at Kilmalkedar, co. Kerry.[2]

[1] The only similar feature I remember to have seen in a church out of Ireland is at Patrixbourne, near Canterbury, which is of Norman date, and has two sculptured lions projecting eastward from the end wall of the chancel at each side of the gable.

[2] Other examples occur at Leabba' Mollagga, co. Cork; St. Caimin's, Iniscaltra; Tempul Macduach and Kill Enda, Aran Islands; Clonamery, co. Kilkenny; Tomgraney, co. Clare; Dulane, co. Meath; St. Cronan's, Roscrea, co. Tipperary; the cathedral at Glendalough, co. Wicklow.

In later times, when Norman details were introduced, the corners of the buildings were ornamented with a round column terminating at the top in a cushion capital, supporting a corner corbel projecting at right angles to the gable walls, of the type already described as at Temple-na-hue, Ardfert, co. Kerry ; and at Tomgraney, co. Clare.

Having shown the general character of the earliest form of church consisting of a nave and chancel in Ireland, we will now endeavour to trace the development of the different architectural features. The chancel arch at Glendalough is of the simplest possible shape, having no mouldings and no impost.[1] At St. Flannan's, Killaloe, co. Clare, we see the next step in advance, for here the semi-circular arch is separated from the jambs by means of a chamfered impost. Finally, in the twelfth century the arch was broken up into several orders of mouldings, each springing from a column in the recesses of the jamb. The table on p. 98 gives the dimensions of the best specimens of chancel arches now existing in Ireland nearly all of which are of the Norman period.

The jambs of some of the chancel arches are inclined like those of the doorways, and occasionally the span of the arch is made greater than the width between the jambs, as at Weir, in Orkney. Most of the later chancel arches in Ireland are elaborately ornamented with sculpture of human heads, having plaited beards of interlaced work of various kinds,

---

[1] There is a similar one, 8 ft. 8 in. wide at the Saints' Church, on Inchagoile, Lough Corrib, co. Galway.
[2] As also at Oughtamama, co. Clare.

and of key patterns. They only differ from the
round-headed doorways in being of a greater size.

	Span of innermost arch.		Height to crown of innermost arch.	
	ft.	in.	ft.	in.
St. Flannan's, Killaloe, co. Clare ...	4	6	8	6
Kilmalkedar, co. Kerry	5	4	8	3
Temple Finghin, Clonmacnois, King's County	6	0	8	4
Saints' Church, Inchagoile, Lough Corrib, co. Galway	8	8	8	8
Trinity Church, Glendalough, co. Wicklow	9	0	10	6
Nuns' Church, Clonmacnois	9	2	12	0
St. Caimin's, Iniscaltra, Lough Derg, co. Clare	10	0	10	0
Rathain, King's County	...		10	2
Monastery Church, Glendalough ...	10	0	11	0
Monaincha, co. Tipperary	7	3	11	9
Cormac's Chapel, Rock of Cashel, co. Tipperary	8	0	12	0
Tuam Cathedral	20	6	19	5
Oughtamama, co. Clare	10	0	13	0

The windows of the Irish churches were not
intended to be glazed, and consequently the great
object was to construct an opening which would let
in as much light as possible, and yet keep out the
rain and wind. This was effected by making the
outer aperture extremely small, with deep splays on
the inner side. The windows are of three kinds,
flat-headed, round-headed, and those with triangular
heads, but in all cases the jambs are inclined. The
flat-headed is perhaps the oldest type as it is found
in the dry-built oratories of Skellig Mhichel, on Oilen
Tsenaig, St. Brendan's, Inisglora, and at Kilmalkedar.
In later times, however, it is less common, except in

the round towers. Of the round-headed windows the most primitive specimen is in the east wall of the oratory of Gallarus, county Kerry. It is built of five stones only, one for the cill and each jamb, and two for the head.[1] The tops of the exteriors of these round-headed windows are not arched, but scooped out of a single block of stone, and the interiors, either constructed in the same way as the exteriors, as at St. Mac Dara's oratory, off the coast of Galway ; or covered over with a flat lintel as at Termon Chronain, county Clare ; or arched, as at Trinity Church, Glendalough. In the later examples, as at St. Caimin's, Iniscaltra, county Clare, and Ratass, county Kerry, the outline of the window is emphasised by a bead moulding running round the whole. The chief difference between the windows in the Irish churches and those in the Norman ones, is that the latter are much longer, the former approximating to a round hole in the wall, and the latter to a slit. The only windows in England at all resembling the Irish ones are at Jarrow, co. Durham.

The latest development of the window in Ireland was to increase its length, and add to the number of the mouldings. A good example of this is to be seen at Banagher, county Londonderry. The east windows of the chancel were also made double in Norman times, as at Temple Righ, Clonmacnois ; Kilmacduagh, county Clare ; Inismaine, county Mayo ; and elsewhere.

---

[1] One stone is generally used for the head, as at S₁. Enda's Church, Aran, where the round-headed east window is built of four stones.

The tops of the triangular-headed windows are either formed of two stones leaning towards each other, as at Cill Cananach, Aran Islands, or cut out of stones lying in horizontal courses, as at Trinity Church, Glendalough. The triangular-headed windows are common both to the Saxon and to the Irish Romanesque style, and in the later examples are ornamental, with a moulding forming a projecting frame all round, as in the round tower at Timahoe, Queen's County.

The doorways of the Irish churches are of two classes, those with a horizontal lintel, and those with a semi-circular arch. The horizontal lintel and the inclining jamb were borrowed from the Pagan style of architecture existing in Ireland before the introduction of Christianity, and even after the arch had superseded the flat lintel the inclining jambs were still preserved. The flat-headed doorways of the most archaic type, found first in the Pagan forts, and then in the dry-built stone-roofed Christian oratories, have been already described in a previous chapter. They are simply openings straight through the walls with a flat top, sloping sides, and entirely devoid of ornament. Architectural dignity was given to these doorways either by sculpturing the lintel, or by running an architrave moulding round the whole. As examples of sculpture on the lintel, we have the cross above the doorways of the churches of St. Fechin, at Fore, county Westmeath, on Ardoilean, off the coast of Galway, at Clonamery, county Kilkenny, at Teach Molaise, on Inismurray, Our Lady's Church, Glendalough, and Killiney, county

Dublin; also above the doorway of the round tower
at Antrim. The crucifixion is carved on the lintel
of the doorways of the church at Maghera, county
Londonderry; and over the doorways of the round
towers at Donaghmore, county Meath; Teghadoe,
co. Kildare; and Brechin, Forfarsh. The simplest
kind of architrave moulding is a projection of rectangular section, as at Ratass, co. Kerry; or Our
Lady's Church, Glendalough. At Temple Martin,
co. Kerry, the moulding is incised, instead of being
in relief. The doorway at Banagher, co. Londonderry, has a flat lintel and an elaborate projecting
architrave on the outside, but a semi-circular arch
within; and at St. Kevin's, Glendalough, there is
a relieving arch above the lintel, showing the style of
the arch and the entablature existing side by side.
The transition from one to the other appears to have
taken place gradually, there being several intermediate forms; at first the round-headed doorway
was made like the early windows, with a single stone
at the top, having a semi-circular hollow scooped out
in it, as in the church of St. Dairbhile, co. Mayo;
and in the round towers at Killree, co. Kilkenny,
and Glendalough, co. Wicklow; then come those
in which a similar hollow is scooped out of three
stones, laid in horizontal courses, as in the round
towers at Monasterboice, co. Louth; next, the
hollow is scooped out of three stones with radiating
joints, as in the round towers at Donaghmore, co.
Meath; and Roscrea, co. Tipperary; lastly, we get
the true arch, built up of several voussoirs, as in the
round tower at Cashel, co. Tipperary. In most

of these instances, although the lintel is discarded in favour of the arch, the sloping jambs and architrave moulding running round the whole are still preserved.

The chief difference between the early Romanesque of Ireland and the Norman style is that in the latter the separation between the arch and the jamb by means of the abacus is far more complete and the architectural treatment of the two parts of the doorway is entirely different, the arch being enriched with mouldings, but the jamb with columns. In the doorway of the round tower at Clonmacnois the arch is separated from the jamb by a square abacus, but there are no decorative features of any kind. Far the finest specimen of a highly-ornamented doorway is in the round tower at Timahoe, Queen's County.[1] Here both the arch and the jamb are broken up into different orders of mouldings, one recessed beyond the other, but instead of filling in the angles of the jambs with nook shafts, as would be done in Norman architecture, the appearance of columns is partially given by V-shaped groovings and roll mouldings, and for the capitals of the columns is substituted a horizontal band of sculptured heads with plaited hair and beards.

Although the arch mouldings are different from those of the jamb, the horizontal band of sculpture which divides the two is in such low relief that the general effect is rather that produced by a doorway surrounded by a continuous architrave rather than

[1] The only other highly-ornamented doorway of a round tower is at Kildare.

one of the Norman type. There is another beautiful doorway of the same kind as the one at Timahoe, and in the Saints' Church on Inchagoil, Lough Corrib, co. Galway. In both these cases the horizontal band of sculpture corresponding to the capitals of the columns in Norman architecture is in one course of stones, but at Killeshin, co. Carlow, the twelfth-century style of England is more nearly approached by the addition of an abacus moulding above the band of sculpture. Dr. Petrie[1] assigns a pre-Norman date to the introduction of the highly-decorated Romanesque style into Ireland, and Miss Margaret Stokes,[2] following in his footsteps, tells us that fifty years before the erection of Westminster Abbey by Edward the Confessor, in 1066, the Church of St. Caimin on Iniscaltra on Lough Derg, co. Clare, was built by King Brian Boruma, and that this building marks the transition to the enriched round-arch style of Ireland. Sir Gilbert Scott, however, finally disposes of this view in his "Lectures on Mediæval Architecture,"[3] in the following passage referring to Dr. Petrie's theories :—" I cannot quite agree with him where Norman details appear ; for though a system of ornamentation may appear in a particular country, it is impossible that it should anticipate the precise forms elaborated much later by a regular course of progression elsewhere." One of the most reliably dated buildings in Ireland is Cormac's Chapel on the Rock of Cashel, co. Tipperary, erected since 1127

[1] "Ecclesiastical Architecture of Ireland," p. 240.
[2] "Early Christian Art in Ireland," p. 179.
[3] Vol. ii. p. 23.

by King Cormac M'Carthy, which is in the Norman style, hardly differing at all from that of England. The principal doorways of the Irish churches and round towers are always either arched or have a flat lintel, but in some of the round towers, as at Roscrea, co. Tipperary ; Devenish, co. Fermanagh ; Iniscaltra, co. Clare ; Timahoe, Queen's County ; and Monasterboice, co. Louth, there is a sort of second doorway above the lower one having a triangular head formed of two stones inclined towards each other. On the inside, however, the aperture is generally arched.

Projecting stones having holes bored through them for the door pivots to turn in or for fixing a wooden lintel exist in the oratories at Kilmalkedar and Gallarus, co. Kerry ; St. Brendan's, Inisglora ; in the churches of St. Caimin, Aran ; Oughtamama, co. Clare ; Agha and Killeshin, co. Carlow ; and St. Kevin's, Glendalough. In the round tower at Roscrea, co. Tipperary, the bolt-holes, pivot stones, and reveal for the door still remain. The Irish churches of the pre-Norman period seldom had more than one door, and it was generally in the west wall of the nave. Porches were quite unknown.

It has already been mentioned that one of the peculiarities of the ecclesiastical settlements in Ireland is the way in which the buildings are arranged in groups. In most other countries in Europe, when a church is found insufficient to accommodate an increased number of worshippers, it was either enlarged or pulled down and rebuilt, but in Ireland a different method was adopted, and a second or third church was erected side by side with the original one instead. Thus it happens that in many places we have the oratory of the saint who founded the establishment in the first instance, perhaps as early as the sixth century, together with a series of later buildings dating down to the fourteenth century.

The settlements of the period we are now dealing with, from A.D. 600 to 1066, differ from the island monasteries, such as the one on Skellig Mhichel, off the coast of Kerry, described in a previous chapter, in having a greater number of churches of various ages, in the substitution of a mere boundary wall for the enclosing cashel, and in the addition of two entirely new features, namely, a round tower and an elaborately-sculptured cross. As a typical monastic establishment of this kind we may take the celebrated one at Clonmacnois, on the banks of the Shannon, in King's County, ten miles below Athlone, which was founded by St. Ciaran, A.D. 544, and was for several centuries the most important seat of learning and art in Ireland. The remains consist of seven churches, two round towers, three sculptured crosses, and a very large number of inscribed sepulchral slabs marking the burial-place of a long line of saints, ecclesiastics, scholars, scribes, princes, and kings. The whole of the buildings are surrounded by a boundary wall enclosing an irregular ten-sided polygonal area, about 450 ft. in diameter.[1] The typical features of the churches have already been pointed out, and the crosses and sepulchral

[1] For plans and illustrations of the churches at Clonmacnois, see works on Irish architecture by Petrie, Rolt Brash, and Lord Dunraven.

slabs will be dealt with subsequently in their proper place, so that the only structures which remain to be described are the round towers. Their origin and use was for a long time a matter of dispute, but Dr. Petrie's masterly essay on the subject gave the *coup de grâce* to all the absurd theories of their connexion with Paganism or Buddhism, and it is now generally admitted that they were erected by the ecclesiastical communities of Ireland during the period between the end of the ninth and the beginning of the twelfth century, chiefly in order to provide a place of safety for the monks and their valuables, whilst the surrounding country was being plundered by the heathen Northmen. The earliest reference to a " cloigtech " (belfry) or round tower in the Irish Annals is under the date 950, but the age of this type of structure can be approximately fixed by the architectural features, which belong to the transition period, between the primitive flat-lintelled style and the round-arched highly-decorated Irish Romanesque.[1]

The ecclesiastical origin of the round towers is conclusively proved by their being invariably associated with churches, and in the later examples actually forming a part of the church itself. Miss Margaret Stokes has collected together all the passages in the Irish Annals mentioning belfries, one of which may be here quoted as a sample of the rest :—

"A.D. 948. The belfry (cloigtech) of Slaine was

[1] Miss Margaret Stokes's "Early Christian Architecture in Ireland," p. 109.

burnt by the foreigners, with its full of relics and distinguished persons, together with Caineachair, Lector of Slane, and the crozier of the patron saint, and a bell, the best of bells " (Annals of the Four Masters).

Miss Stokes also gives a map of Ireland in her " Early Christian Architecture of Ireland," showing that the round towers are most thickly distributed in the parts of the country known to have been ravaged by the Northmen. There are at present seventy-six round towers remaining in Ireland, of which thirteen are perfect, or very nearly so, and the remainder in varying states of preservation. There are three round towers in Scotland [1] whose presence there is to be accounted for by the continual intercourse which went on between the Churches of the two countries after the mission of St. Colomba to Iona in A.D. 565.

Dr. E. A. Freeman,[2] in a brilliant passage, points out that the bell tower is the peculiar property of the Christian Church, and attributes its introduction to the Lombardic architects of Northern Italy. He says : —" It is to Christian worship alone that the joyful sound of bells gathers the multitude of the faithful ; it is therefore to Christian temples only that the lofty towers are attached, which rear them on high to convey their clear voice more distinctly and uninter-

[1] At Brechin, Forfarshire ; Abernethy, Fifeshire ; Egilsay, and Deerness in Orkney, the latter now destroyed (see Dr. J. Anderson's " Scotland in Early Christian Times," 1st series, lecture 2).

[2] " History of Architecture," p. 182. The earliest historical statement about a bell tower describes the erection of one at St. Peter's in Rome, A.D. 780, by Pope Stephen III.

ruptedly. The use of bell involved that of belfries, as a matter of necessity; having thus its origin in real use, and no classical models existing to mislead the architects, the belfry, unlike most other features, rose at once, not, indeed, into its full perfection, but to a very considerable degree of excellence. Indeed, there is no kind of edifice on which more care was bestowed throughout the Romanesque and Gothic periods, or in which the respective peculiarities and beauties of the successive styles are more clearly marked. It is not merely in the details that this is shown, but every period, every country, almost every district, has its own peculiar form of steeple, and that, in nearly every case, its most beautiful and most distinguishing feature."

The existence of ecclesiastical round towers on the Continent at Ravenna, at St. Maurice Epinal, in Lorraine, and elsewhere, gives support to the theory that those found in Ireland are merely survivals in a remote locality of a type which was once common all over Europe.

The Irish round towers are, in the majority of cases, detached from the church like the Italian campanile, but in the later examples, as at Temple Finghin, Clonmacnois, and Egilsay, in Orkney, they are built against the church, and at St. Kevin's, Glendalough, the tower is reduced to a diminutive size, and placed on the top of the gable.

The isolated round towers are circular in plan, diminishing in diameter towards the top, so that the walls have a regular batter all the way up, and terminate in a conical roof. There is generally a projecting plinth at the base, just above the ground level. The interior is divided into five or six stories, there being either set-offs in the masonry or corbels to support the floors.

The openings consist of a door, from 5 ft. to 6 ft. high, and 2 ft. to 3 ft. wide, placed at an average height of 12 ft. above the level of the ground, so as to be inaccessible without a ladder ; a single window in each story, except the top one, which has four facing the cardinal points.[1]

In some of the round towers the opening in the second story is of greater size than the others, and is more like a door than a window. It may possibly have been used as a door in times of danger, being more inaccessible than the lower one in consequence of its greater height from the ground. The architectural details of the towers correspond with those of the churches of the same period. The conical roofs remain quite perfect in a few of the towers, that at Temple Finghin, at Clonmacnois, having the stones arranged herring-bone fashion.

At Ardmore the cap-stone is still in existence, with a socket for the insertion of a finial, or a cross. Miss Stokes has endeavoured to detect four different styles of building in the Irish round towers, but local conditions, such as the class of material available and the skill of the workmen in the district, are so variable that any classification of the kind must necessarily be more or less unsatisfactory.

[1] Except at Temple Finghin, Clonmacnois, where there are two ; at Kilmacduagh, co. Galway, six ; and at O'Rorke's tower, Clonmacnois, and Tulloherin, co. Kilkenny, eight.

The details of the doors and windows afford the surest criterion as to date. Towers like that at Antrim having a flat-headed doorway, and no mouldings are probably the oldest ; then come those with a doorway, having a round head hollowed out of one, two, or three stones, and surrounded entirely by an architrave moulding ; and, lastly, the most advanced type has a round-headed doorway, with a rue arch and abacus, as in O'Rorke's tower at Clonmacnois, which there is documentary evidence to show was completed by Gillachrist-Na-Maeleoin, and Toirdhealbhach-Ua-Conchobhair in A.D. 1124.

The masonry varies a good deal, from the coarse, open-jointed work at Antrim to the carefully-dressed ashlar laid in even courses at Ardmore, co. Waterford ; but the most characteristic Irish masonry is to be seen at Kilmacduach, co. Galway, consisting of Cyclopean work, neatly fitted together with the beds inclining at different angles instead of being horizontal, and sometimes with the corner of one block notched out to receive a smaller stone. Sculptured details exist in the round towers at Ardmore, co. Waterford ; Devenish, co. Fermanagh ; Donaghmore, co. Meath ; Kildare ; Timahoe, Queen's County ; Antrim ; Teachdoe, co. Kildare ; and Brechin, Forfarshire.

The following table, compiled from Lord Dunraven and Dr. Petrie's works, gives the dimensions of the best-preserved round towers in Ireland and Scotland :—

Place.	County.	Height.	Diameter at base inside.	Thickness of walls.	Height of doorways above ground.
IN PERFECT	**PRESERVATION.**				
		ft.	ft.	ft.	ft.
Antrim	Antrim	92.0	9.0	3.0	7.6
Ardmore ...	Waterford ...	95.0	9.5	3.4½	13.0
Cashel	Tipperary ...	80.0	8.0	4.0	12.0
Clondalkin ...	Dublin	85.9	7.4	3.10	13.0
Clonmacnois ...	King's County	56.0	8.0	3 0	—
(Temple Finghin.)					
Devenish ...	Fermanagh ...	84.10	8.0	4.0	9.0
Killala	Mayo	84.0	9.0	3.6	11.0
Kilmacduach	Galway	120.0	10.0	4.0	26.0
Rattoo	Kerry	92.0	7.4	3.10	—
Timahoe ...	Queen's County	96.0	10.0	4.4	15.0
Brechin	Forfar	106.6	7.11	3.8	6.3
NOT QUITE	**PERFECT.**				
Abernethy ...	Fife	72.0	8·0	3.6	2.6
Clonmacnois ...	King's Co. ...	62.0	11.0	3.9	—
(O'Rourke'sTow'r)					
Disert Ængus	Limerick ...	67.0	9.0	4.3	15.0
Disert O'Dea	Clare	50.0	10.2	5.0	13.0
Egilsay	Orkney	48.0	7.0	3.6	—
Glendalough ...	Wicklow ...	110.0	8.6	—	10.0
Iniscaltra ...	Clare	80.0	7.10	3.5	10.7
Monasterboice	Louth	110.0	8.9	3.0	4.0
Roscrea	Tipperary ...	80.0	8.3	4.0	9.9

Sepulchral and other Monuments.

The sepulchral monuments of the earlier Christian Celtic period, before A.D. 600, it will be remembered, consisted of rude unhewn stones with inscriptions in debased Latin capitals or in Oghams; those of the later period, from A.D. 600 to 1066, are elaborately sculptured, and have inscriptions in minuscules, or small letters. The oldest MSS., as well as the oldest inscribed stones, are written in capital letters, all of the same size; but as books became more common it was necessary to devise new forms of letters which could be drawn with fewer strokes of the pen, and therefore more rapidly. This was done by rounding off certain parts of a letter so as to reduce two or more strokes to one continuous curve, and also by omitting other parts of a letter with the same object.[1] During this process of development some letters became taller than the rest, having tails above and below the line. The result was that a new style of writing was arrived at, intermediate between capitals and the cursive, or running hand. These new characters are called minuscules, by palæographers, and from them are descended the small letters used for printing at the present day. Each country in Europe had from the seventh to the twelfth century its local variety of minuscule letter, which was accordingly classified as Caroline, Saxon, Hiberno-Saxon, and so on.[2] The change in the style of writing which began as early as the sixth century went on slowly, but continuously, so that it is possible to

---

[1] If, by doing this, the form of the altered letter was made similar to that of another, some further distinguishing mark was required.

[2] For further information see article by E. Maunde Thompson on Palæography in the "Encyclopædia Britannica"; I. O. Westwood's "Palæographia Pictoria Sacra"; and the Palæographical Society's Publications.

date a MSS. or lapidary inscription by comparing the shapes of the letters with those in MSS. of known age. The geographical area to which a MSS. belongs can be determined in a similar way. The general appearance of the minuscules in use in Ireland in the seventh or eighth century may be gathered from an examination of the pillar stone standing outside the western doorway of the Church of Kilmalkedar, co. Kerry.

This monument has on the front an incised cross, with spiral terminations to the arms, and on the side the invocation Dni (contracted for Domini) and a minuscule alphabet of twenty-three letters, or twenty-four with the A at the beginning, which has been broken off.

The transition from capitals to minuscules took place gradually in Wales, Cornwall, and Gaul, in which countries the letters of many of the inscriptions are mixed and exhibit intermediate forms, but in Ireland there is only one inscription in debased Latin capitals, at Killeen Cormac, co. Kildare, all the rest being in minuscules. The inference to be drawn from this is that whilst the Ogham character only was used in Ireland, the minuscule form of letter was being developed out of the Latin capitals in those parts of Great Britain where the inhabitants came in contact with the Romans, and learned from them their methods of writing. None of the stones with minuscule inscriptions found in Ireland can be shown to be older than the seventh century, and as there is only one instance of a stone in that country with an inscription in debased Latin capitals, it is evident that before writing became common there the minuscule form of letter had been fully developed elsewhere. The number of monuments with minuscule inscriptions at present known to exist in Great Britain, is about 317, of which 260 are in Ireland, 12 in England, 3 in Scotland, and 42 in Wales. The monuments upon which these inscriptions occur consist of rude pillar stones, erect crosses, and sepulchral slabs. The pillar stones without any artificial tooling are probably the oldest, for as a general rule the minuscule type of letter indicates an advance in style, and is accompanied by elaborate sculpture and the peculiar Celtic forms of ornament, such as spirals, key patterns, and interlaced work. Some of the crosses and pillar stones are sepulchral, but others are erected in sacred places for devotional, terminal, commemorative, and other purposes.

As a good example of a sepulchral pillar stone, with a minuscule inscription, we may take the one standing in front of the ancient church dedicated to St. Patrick, on the Island of Inchagoile, Lough Corrib, co. Galway. It is about 4 ft. high, and has two incised crosses on the side and two similar crosses on the front, with the following inscription reading from the top downwards :—

"Lie Lugaedon Macci Menueh."
(The stone of Lugaed, Son of Men.)

At Kilnasaggart (the church of the priests), co. Armagh, is a pillar stone, 7 ft. 6 in. high, with a minuscule inscription, which belongs to a different class from the above, being evidently not sepulchral, but dedicatory. On the front of the monument are two incised crosses, one at the top of the plain Latin shape, and one at the bottom with spiral terminations to the arms, and enclosed within a circle. Between the two crosses is the following inscription :—

"In loc so tanimmairini Ternhoc Mac Ceran Bic, Ercul Peter Apstel."
(Ternóc, son of Ciaran the Little, bequeathed this place under the protection of Peter the Apostle.)

On the back are ten circular crosses. The death of Ternóc, son of Ciaran, is recorded in the Annals of Tigemach, under the year A.D. 716.

The absence of sculpture on the pillar stones with minuscule inscriptions is attributable in some cases to early date, as except for the crosses and the forms of the letters there is nothing to differentiate them from the Ogham monoliths. In other cases it may be due to rudeness of workmanship in a remote district. The crosses on the pillar stones with minuscule inscriptions are generally incised and of simple shape, but at Reask, co. Kerry, there is spiral ornament in addition, indicating the first step towards the more highly-decorated style. There are several pillar stones with minuscule inscriptions in Wales, the most interesting specimens being St. Thomas's stone at Court Isaf Farm, near Port Talbot, Glamorganshire; St. Gwnnws' stone at Llanwnnws, near Ystrad Meyric, Cardiganshire; and St. Cadfan's stone at Towyn, Merionethshire.

The most common type of sepulchral monument in Ireland from A.D. 600 to 1066 was a flat slab, with a cross and minuscule inscription carved upon it, placed in a horizontal position over the grave. In Wales sepulchral slabs of this description are rare, and in Cornwall there are only two, but in Ireland about 250 are known to exist, the largest collection being at Clonmacnois, King's County, where there are as many as 177. One of the chief reasons why the cemetery of Clonmacnois is so prolific in sepulchral memorials of celebrated personages is on account of the belief which existed that St. Ciaran, the founder of the monastery in A.D. 544, would have power to intercede with the Deity at the Day of Judgment for those who were buried near him.

In the Bodleian Library at Oxford is preserved an Irish poem written by Enoch O'Gillan, singing the praises of the nobles who claim Clonmacnois as their last resting-place. It commences thus :—

> " Ciaran's city is Cluain-mic-Nois,
> A place dew-bright, red-rosed ;
> Of a race of chiefs whose fame is lasting
> Are hosts under the peaceful clear-streamed place.
>
> Nobles of the children of Conn
> Are under the flaggy, brown sloped cemetery ;
> A knot, or a craebh, over each body,
> And a fair, just, Ogham name." [1]

Many of the flags here described have been destroyed in the course of ages, some, alas! quite recently, but Miss M. Stokes has published illustrations of 177 from drawings made by the late Dr.

[1] Mr. Wm. M. Hennessy's translation in Petrie's " Christian Inscriptions in the Irish Language," edited by Miss M. Stokes.

Petrie. One only of the slabs corresponds exactly with the words of the poem in having "a fair just Ogham name" upon it, but the knot or interlaced work occurs on several. The great value of the collection of early tombstones at Clonmacnois is that we have here, what is to be found nowhere else in Great Britain, a series of eighty-one monuments, dated, from historical evidence by means of the names mentioned in the inscriptions, between A.D. 600 and 1400. Of these,—

4 belong to the	7th century.
6 ,, ,,	8th ,,
28 ,, ,,	9th ,,
18 ,, ,,	10th ,,
18 ,, ,,	11th ,,
6 ,, ,,	12th ,,
1 ,, ,,	13th ,,

The names include many of the successors of St. Ciaran as abbots and bishops of Clonmacnois ; kings of Ulster, Leinster, and Connaught ; lords of Teffia and Hy-Many ; men of learning of European reputation, such as Suibine Mac Maelhumai, "Scotorum Sapientissimus," and St. Fiachra, whose memory is still perpetuated in the French word "fiacre." In addition to the names which have been identified there are a great many more about whom nothing whatever is known.

In other parts of Ireland there are about 177 more sepulchral slabs with minuscule inscriptions, the names mentioned on 57 of which correspond with those mentioned in history.[1] One of the

[1] See table given in Petrie's "Christian Inscriptions in the Irish Language," vol. ii. p. 179.

most interesting of these is the tombstone of St. Berechtir, of Tullylease, who died A.D. 839, as it affords one of the best examples of a reliably dated stone with Celtic forms of ornament. The minuscule inscriptions found on sepulchral slabs in Ireland are, with few exceptions, in the Irish language. The most common formula is, " ōr do " or " ōr ar," meaning "a prayer for," followed by the name of the deceased in the genitive case ; " ōr " is the contraction for " oroit," and it is occasionally written at full length, but not often ; " do " is in a few cases spelt " du," and once omitted altogether. The word " anmain " (soul) is sometimes added, or " bendacht" (blessing) put in place of " oroit."

The following table shows the relative frequency with which the various formulæ occur :—

Ōr do	...	...	94	Ōr ar ...	...	13
Ōrt do ...	...	...	1	Ōro ar ...	...	1
Ōroit do	...	...	2	Ōroit ar	...	10
Ōr du ...	...	...	4	Ōr ar anmain ...	...	1
Ōr ...	...	...	1	Ōroit ar anmain...	...	2

Bendacht ar anmain ... 3

On a large proportion of the slabs the name of the deceased only is given in the nominative case, without prefix of any kind.

Usually the first name occurs alone in the inscriptions, but in a certain number the surname is added, as, for example, at Clonmacnois,—

" Ōr do Bran U Caillen."
(Pray for Bran O'Caillen.)

And,—

> "Ōroit do Conaing Mac Conghail."
> (Pray for Conaing son of Conghal.)

The names are nearly all those of men, although at Clonard, co. Meath, there is an exception in the tombstone of Meind ingin Meicc Srappan (Mend, the daughter of the son of Srappan).[1]

The following names are followed by a descriptive epithet :—

At Clonmacnois,—
> "*Corbre Crum*" (*Corbre the Bent*),

and "*Colman Bocht*" (*Colman the Poor*).

At Monaincha, co. Tipperary,—
> "*Bran Dub*" (*Bran the Black*).

Occasionally the office or occupation of the deceased is given, as for instance,—

At Clonmacnois,—
> "*Mc Taidg Hui Cellaich, do Rig Humane*" (*Taidg O'Kelly, King of Hy-Many*),
> "*Epscop Dathal*" (*Bishop Dathal*),
> "*Oriacan Eps*" (*Bishop Oriacan*),
> "*Maeliohain Eps*" (*Bishop Maeliohain*).

At St. Brecan's, Aran Môr,—
> "*Bran N'ailither*" (*Bran the Pilgrim*),

and "*Tomas Ap*" (*Thomas, Abbot*).

At Lismore,—
> "*Cormac P.*" (*Cormac, Presbiter*).

The name of the maker of the tombstone is mentioned in the following,—

---

[1] Petrie's "Christian Inscr.," vol. ii. p. 63.

At Clonmacnois,—
"*Ōr do . . . . cillin icandernad in lecsa.*" (*A prayer for
. . . cillin, by whom this stone was made.*)

And,—

"*Oroit ar Thurcain lasan-dernad in Chrossa.*" (*Pray for
Turcain, by whom this cross was made.*)

Particulars are sometimes, but not often, furnished
as to work done by the deceased when alive, as,—

At Termonfechin, co. Louth,—
"+ *Oroit do Ultan & do Dubthach dorigni in Caissel.*"
(+ *Pray for Ultan and for Dubthach, who made the Stone
Fort.*)

In three cases the sepulchral slab marks the grave
of several nameless individuals,—

At Iniscaltra,—
"+ *Ilad in dechenboir.*" (+ *The stone of the ten persons.*)

At St. Brecan's, Aran Môr,—
"*Ōr ar II Canoin.*' (*Pray for the two Canons.*)

And,—

"*VII. Romani.*" (*The Seven Romans.*)

The following inscriptions are in Latin :—

At Reask, co. Kerry,—
"*Dn̄s and Dn̄e* " (*for Dominus and Domine*).

At Kilmalkedar,—
"*Dn̄e*" (*for Domine*).

At St. Brecan's, Aran Môr,—
"*Sci Brecani*" (*St. Brecan*).

At Inismurray,—
"*Crux* " (*Cross*),

and,—

" + *Ōr do Muredach hū Chomochain hic dormit.*" (+ *Pray for Muredach O'Chomocan, who sleeps here.*)

At Brookborough, co. Fermanagh,—

" *Ōr do Dunchad, pspit hic.*" (*Pray for Dunchad, Presbyter here.*)

At Kells,—

"*Patricii et Columbæ Crux.*" (*The Cross of Patrick and Columba.*)

At Tullylease, co. Cork,—

" *Quicumquæ hunc titulum legerit orat pro Berechtuire.*" (*Let whosoever reads this titulus pray for Berechtir.*)

The Christian symbols which occur upon the sepulchral slabs with minuscule inscriptions in Ireland and Wales consist of crosses of various forms, accompanied in one instance[1] by a fish, and in two others[2] by the Alpha and Omega and the monogrammatic contractions for the name of Jesus Christ in Greek letters.

The last class of monuments with minuscule inscriptions to be considered are erect crosses, richly sculptured with figure subjects and Celtic ornament. These differ from the rude pillar stones described in the previous chapters, (1) in being shaped into the form of the cross instead of having a cross incised upon the face; (2) in having the shaft mortised into a socket-stone at the base, and sometimes having the head made in a separate piece and mortised into the top of the shaft; (3) in being covered with a profusion of sculpture in relief

---

[1] At Fuerty, co. Roscommon.

[2] At Tullylease, co. Cork, and Glendalough, co. Wicklow.

arranged in panels, inclosed in a bead or cable moulding; (4) in having the inscription carved in small letters reading horizontally instead of in capitals reading vertically; (5) in the formulæ of the inscriptions being more varied, and the names of a later type.

The inscriptions afford the best data for determining the age of these monuments. On almost every religious site of any importance in Ireland a cross of large size was erected, varying in height from 10 to 20 feet. Some of the crosses were plain, but there are still in existence at least thirty specimens, and probably more, which are highly ornamented.[1] Out of these six have minuscule inscriptions as follows :—

At Delgany, co. Wicklow (on the shaft of cross in churchyard),—

"Ōr do Dicul ocus Maelodran Sair."
(Pray for Dicul and Maelodran, the Wright.)

At Kells, co. Meath (on the base of cross in churchyard),—

"Patricii et Columbæ Crux."
(The cross of Patrick and of Columba.)

At Monasterboice, co. Louth (on the bottom of the shaft of one of the crosses in the churchyard),—

"Ōr do Muiredach lasan dernad in chrossa."
(Pray for Muiredach, by whom this cross was made.)

---

[1] Although H. O'Neill, Miss Stokes, and others have written on the subject, no one has taken the trouble to make a complete list of the Irish crosses.

At Clonmacnois, King's County (on two sides of the bottom of the shaft of one of the crosses in the churchyard),—

> "Ōr do Flaind Mc Maelsechlaind."
> (Pray for Fland, son of Maelsechlaind.)
> "Colman dorro ina in croissa ar in Ri Flaind."
> (Colman who made this cross for King Fland.)

At Tuam, co. Galway (on two edges of fragment of shaft of cross preserved inside old parish church),—

> "Ōr don Rig do Thurdelbuch U Chonchobair.
> Ōr dont Haer do Gillucrist U Thuathail."
> (Pray for the King, for Turdelbach O'Conchobar.
> Pray for the Artizan, for Gillachrist O'Tuathal.)

> "Ōr do Chomarba Iarlaithe do Aed U Ossin lasin dernad in Chrossa."
> (Pray for the successor of Iarlath, for Aed O'Oissin, by whom this cross was made.)

(On two sides of the base of the cross in the Market-place),—

> "Ōr do Thoirdelbuch u Chonchobuir dont . . . Iarlathe lasin dernad in sae . . "
> (Pray for Turlogh O'Conor, for the . . . of Iarlathe, by whom this was made . .)
> "Ōr do U Ossin dond Abbaid ; lasan dernad."
> (Pray for O'Hossin for the Abbot, by whom this was made.)

Out of the persons here mentioned the following have been identified, thus enabling the dates of the crosses to be approximately fixed : — Muiredach, abbot of Monasterboice, who erected the cross at that place, and died in A.D. 924 ; Colman, abbot of Clonmacnois, who made the cross there, and died in A.D. 924; Fland Mac Maelsechlain, king of Ireland, for whom the cross at Clonmacnois was made, and who died in A.D. 914; Aed O'Oissin, archbishop of Tuam, under whose direction the cross at that place was made by Gillachrist O'Tuathal, and who died A.D. 1161; and Turlogh O'Conor, king of Connaught, who died A.D. 1156.

The cross at Kells is evidently not sepulchral, as SS. Patrick and Columba are known to have been buried elsewhere, and to have died at a period long anterior to the introduction of the ornamental forms with which the cross is sculptured. The cross at Clonmacnois is referred to in the Annals of the Four Masters as the "high cross" (under the date A.D. 957), and as the "Cross of the Scriptures" (under the date A.D. 1060). The latter designation refers to the Crucifixion and other Bible subjects represented in the sculpture with which the monument is adorned. It is evident that the more important crosses found in Ireland were erected for devotional purposes upon the most sacred spots, and that the usual form of sepulchral stone was a simple slab, marked with the symbol of the Christian faith, and laid flat upon the grave of the deceased.

There are in Wales about 64 stones with Celtic forms of ornament, 27 of which have minuscule inscriptions. Out of these 64 stones 24 are erect crosses, resembling those occurring in Ireland in many respects, but being generally of smaller dimensions; the remainder are either sepulchral slabs or upright pillars. In the absence of an inscription giving definite information as to the manner in which

a stone, having sculpture on one side only, was intended to be placed, it is often difficult to ascertain
whether it originally lay horizontally or was erected
vertically. The height of the Welsh crosses varies
from 6 ft. to 14 ft., those at Carew and Nevern, in Pembrokeshire, and the Maen Achwynfan, in Flintshire,
being the tallest. The forms of the crosses vary,
but the most typical shape is the round-headed or
" wheel " cross. Of the 64 Welsh stones with Celtic
ornament 42 occur in the counties of Glamorganshire
and Pembrokeshire, so that it would appear there was
an intimate connexion between Ireland and South
Wales in early times. The stones which are both
ornamented and inscribed exist at the following
places :—

Glamorganshire.—Margam (5), Llantwit Major (3), Coy-
church (2), Merthyr Mawr (2), Kenfig, Bryn Keffneithan,
Baglan, Llandough.

Pembrokeshire.—Nevern, Penally, Carew, Pen Arthur, St.
David's.

Brecknockshire.—Llandevaelog Vach, Llanthetty, Llanhamllech, Llanfrynach.

Cardiganshire.—Llanwnnws.

Denbighshire.—Eliseg's Pillar, near Valle Crucis.

Caermarthenshire.—Llanarthney.

The formulæ of the inscriptions on the Welsh
stones are generally longer than those on the Irish
crosses and sepulchral slabs, and the Latin language is used almost exclusively instead of the
vernacular. In the latter the name of the deceased
only is given, with the prefix " ōr do " (a prayer for),
but in Wales the name of the erector is added, and
it is also stated that the monument is put up for the

soul of the dead in the name of One or all Three of the Persons of the Trinity.

In the earlier minuscule inscriptions the monument is called a stone and not a cross, as is most common subsequently. Thus at Newborough in Anglesey there is a pillar 5 ft. high, without sculpture or any Christian symbol, inscribed :—

> ". . . cini erexit hunc lapidem." [1]
> (. . . cini erected this stone.)

And then at Llanhamllech, Brecknockshire, there is a slab with a cross, figures, and Celtic ornament, inscribed,—

> "Johannis Moridic surexit hunc lapidem."
> (John Moridic erected this stone.)

In the inscription on the cross shaft at Llantwit Major, Glamorganshire, "crucem" is substituted for "lapidem" and "pro anima" is added, as follows :—

> " + Samson posuit hanc crucem pro anima ejus +."
> (Samson placed this cross for his soul.)

Also on one of the crosses at Margam, in Glamorganshire, we have,—

> "Crux XPI + Enniaun pro anima Guogoret fecit."
> (The Cross of Christ + Enniaun made it for the soul of Guogoret.)

The names of the First two Persons of the Trinity are introduced in the following, on one of the crosses at Margam :—

---

[1] The Latin inscriptions are given with all their barbarous inaccuracies.

(No. 5.)　Cross of Grutne and Ahest at Margam, with
Inscription in Minuscules.
(From a rubbing by J. R. ALLEN.)
Scale ⅛ real size.　　　　*p.* 127.

" In nomine Di Sumi Crux Critidi proparabit Grutne pro anima Ahest."

(In the name of the most High God, Grutne prepared this Cross of Christ for the soul of Ahest.)

And on one of the crosses at Llantwit Major the Third Person of the Trinity is also mentioned :—

" In nomine di Patris et Speretus Sancdi sanc crucem Houelt properabit pro anima Res patres ejus."

(In the name of God the Father and of the Holy Spirit, Howel prepared this cross for the soul of Rees his father.)

On another of the crosses at Llantwit Major the formula is :—

" In nomine di Summi incipit Crux Salvatoris quæ preparavit Samsoni pro anima sua et pro anima Iuthahelo Rex et pro Artmali tecan × ."

(In the name of the Most High God this cross was begun, which Samson prepared for his soul, and for the soul of King Ithael and for Arthmael.)

On an upright stone with an ornamental cross upon it, at Llanwnnws, Cardiganshire, is an inscription of an entirely different kind from the foregoing, and corresponding very nearly with that on the tombstone of St. Berechtir of Tullylease, co. Cork, aready mentioned. It reads :—

" XPS Quicunque explicaverit hoc nomen det benedixionem pro anima Hiroidil filius Carotinn."

(XPS. Whosoever shall explain this name let him give a blessing for the soul of Hiroidil, son of Carotin.)

One of the earliest instances of the supplication of prayers for the soul of the deceased is on the Ogham inscribed pillar on Caldy Island in Pembrokeshire. This monument has, in addition to the Oghams, an incised cross on the face, and below it the following inscription in mixed capitals and minuscules :—

" Et singno crucis in illam fingsi.
Oro omnibus ambulantibus ibi exorent pro anima Catuoconi."
(And I placed the sign of the cross upon it.
I beg from all passers-by that they may pray for the soul of Catuocon.)

A list of about forty-seven proper names is to be collected from the Welsh stones with minuscule inscriptions, but the number which have been identified is very small. The names Iltet and Samson occurring on the crosses at Llantwit have been supposed to be intended for Iltutus, the founder of the monastery at this place in the fifth century, and Samson his contemporary; but the style of the art of the monuments is that of a much later period. A more probable suggestion identifies the Samson, Howell ap Rhys, and Arthmael, mentioned in the Llantwit inscriptions, with persons living in the ninth century. The " Catamanus Rex Sapientissimus Opinatissimus Omnium Regum" of the Llangadwaladr inscribed stone in Anglesey is perhaps Catman or Cadfan, who lived in the seventh century. A complete catalogue of all the names found on the Welsh inscribed stones is given in Prof. Westwood's " Lapidarium Walliæ," and their meaning, &c., is discussed in Prof. J. Rhys's " Lectures on Welsh Philology."

In England there are crosses with Celtic forms of ornament and minuscule inscriptions, which may be classed with those in Ireland and Wales, at Trevillet, Lanherne, and St. Neot, in Cornwall; at Hawkswell, Yarm, and Dewsbury, in Yorkshire; and at Beckermet St. Bridget's, in Cumberland. Cross slabs with minuscule inscriptions exist in England at Camborne and Pendarves, in Cornwall; and Hartlepool and Billingham, in county Durham.

The inscriptions at Dewsbury and Yarm are in ancient Northumbrian dialect, and will be referred to when dealing with the monuments of the Saxon Church, but the others are in Latin, with formulæ like those on the Welsh stones, the following being typical specimens :—

On the base of the cross at St. Neot,—

> " Doniert rogavit pro anima."
> (Doniert prayed for the soul.)

On the back and front shaft of the cross at Trevillet,—

> " Aelnat fecit hanc crucem pro anima sua."
> (Aelnat made this cross for his soul.)
> "Matheus, Marcus, Lucas, Johannis."
> (Matthew, Mark, Luke, John.)

On the shaft of the cross at Hawkswell,—

> " Hæc est crux Sci Jacobi."
> (This is the cross of St. James.)

On the cross slab at Camborne,—

> " Leviut jussit hec altare pro anima sua."
> (Leviut ordered this altarstone for his soul.)

On the cross slab at Billingham,—

> "Orate pro . . . "   (Pray for . . .)

K

It is a curious fact that although Scotland is so rich in sculptured crosses of the pre-Norman period, hardly any of them are inscribed ; and there is only one with minuscules upon it at St. Vigean's, in Forfarshire. This inscription appears to contain the names Drosten and Forcus, but its true meaning has not been yet discovered.

Portable Objects.

The portable objects belonging to the Celtic Church consist of books, bells, and croziers, generally enclosed in metal shrines ; reliquaries, chalices, altar vessels, metal plaques with Scripture subjects, processional crosses, and leather book satchels. These relics are of great interest, not only on account of the extreme beauty of the ornamental features, which will be discussed more fully in a subsequent chapter, but also because they exhibit special characteristics not found elsewhere, and are, in most cases, associated with the name of the saint to whom they originally belonged. The vicissitudes through which the relics passed in the course of centuries were often of a most romantic description. The story was generally the same. The book, bell, or crozier, belonging to the founder of the church, was supposed to have acquired peculiar sanctity and even supernatural properties by association with him, and after his death was often enclosed in a costly metal shrine of exquisite workmanship. Each relic had its hereditary custodian, who was answerable for its safe keeping, and who in return received certain privileges, such as power to collect dues from the parishioners, the title to inherit land of which the relic constituted the tenure, the right to levy fees for the use of the shrine, independence of all authority respecting its possession or anything concerning it, and protection from harm whilst carrying it through a hostile country.

The relics of early Celtic saints were used chiefly for curing diseases, for taking oaths upon, and for recovering stolen property. When lent for such purposes a deposit had to be made as a guarantee for its safe return, and a fee paid to its keeper. A few of the Celtic bells are still in the churches of the saints to whom they originally belonged; but most of the enshrined bells, croziers, and books have been either stolen on account of the value of their gold and silver mountings, or sold by their keepers when tempted by the offer of some rich collector.

During the terrible invasions of the Northmen in the ninth and tenth centuries, the trembling monks took their treasures for greater safety to the stronghold in the round tower beside the church, there, perhaps, to be burnt by a relentless foe, or buried them with but faint chance of ever returning to recover their property. If a shrine escaped the robberies and conflagrations of this period it may be that it suffered no further violence until after the Reformation; but when the protection of the Church became feeble, and feelings of reverence disappeared, the hereditary keeper no longer remaining true to his trust, sold that which in a previous generation he would only have parted with at the expense of his life. Fortunately, many of the finest shrines in Ireland fell into the hands of antiquaries like Dr. Petrie, who bequeathed them to the nation, and they are now to be seen in the Museum of the Royal Irish Academy. The ecclesiastical objects found in Scotland have similarly gravitated at last to the Museum of Antiquities in Edinburgh. A few others are in the British Museum and private collections.

The age of many of the relics of the Celtic Church has been ascertained by inscriptions upon them giving the names of persons known in history, and the pedigrees of some of them can be traced back to a very remote period by references to the shrines, and their keepers in the Irish Annals and other documents. Take for instance of the shrine of the Bell of St. Patrick's Will, which has an Irish inscription in minuscules, of which the following is a translation :—

"Pray for Domnall O'Loughlin, by whom this bell was made, and for Cathalán O'Maelchalland, the keeper of this bell, and for Cúdulig O'Inmainen with his sons, who covered it."

The Donnell O'Lochlain here mentioned was king of Ireland, A.D. 1083 to 1121, thus fixing the date of the shrine at the end of the eleventh or beginning of the twelfth century. The bell itself is believed, by Dr. Reeves, to be as old as the time of St. Patrick. It is referred to in the Annals of Ulster, under the date A.D. 552, as being one of the three precious swearing relics found in the tomb of St. Patrick, viz., the relique coach (vial), the Angel's Gospel, and the bell called Clog-an-eadhachta (the Bell of St. Patrick's Will). The "Annals of the

Four Masters" contains the next entry under the
year A.D. 1044, alluding to its profanation (meaning
by the violation of an oath taken upon it), for
which the inhabitants of the barony of Lower
Dundalk and of Cremorne had to pay a heavy
penalty.

The hereditary custodians of the shrine O'Mellan
and Mulholland are mentioned in the same Annals,
under the years A.D. 1356, 1425, and 1441. In 1758
it came into the possession of the last hereditary
custodian, Henry Mulholland, the master of a gram-
mar school, who bequeathed it to a favourite pupil,
named M'Clean. At his death it was sold to the
Rev. J. H. Todd, D.D., for £50, and afterwards
purchased by the Royal Irish Academy, in whose
Museum, in Dublin, it is now preserved. We have
thus been able to trace the authentic history of this
wonderful bell for more than a thousand years, from
the time it was taken from the tomb of St. Patrick by
Columbkill to the present day. The Quirigh of St.
Fillan has an equally interesting record from the
reign of Robert the Bruce, when it was first known to
have been in possession of the Dewars (or hereditary
keepers), until its purchase in 1876, from the last
representative of its ancient keepers, Alexander
Dewar, of Plympton, Canada, by the Society of
Antiquaries of Scotland. The following is a list of
relics whose hereditary keepers are known, and from
whom in most cases they were purchased at a recent
period, either by the museums where they are now
deposited, or by collectors who eventually sold or
bequeathed them to these museums :—

Book Shrines.

Cover of St. Molaise's Gospels	O'Meehan.
,, ,, Columba's Psalter..............	MacRobhartaig.
,, ,, Cairnech's Calendar	O'Morison.

Bell Shrines.

Shrine of Bell of St. Patrick's Will	Mulholland.
,, ,, ,, Colanus..................	Breslin.

Bells.

Black Bell of St. Patrick	MacBeolan.
Bell of Termon MacGuirk.....................	MacGuirk.
,, Drumragh	McEnhills.
,, St. Mogue	Magoveran.
,, Fenagh......................................	O'Rorke.
,, Ballynaback	O'Heany.
,, St. Bodan	Duffy.
,, St. Senan................................	Keane.

Croziers.

Crozier of Dympna..............................	O'Luan.
,, St. Fillan	Dewar.

Many documents are still extant to show that the
possession of relics of the Celtic Church was sufficient
to prove the owner's title to the landed property
which went with it.[1] Thus the keeper of the bell of
Struan, in Strathearn, held three acres of land by
its tenure. A croft of land called Deray Croft of
Banquhori-terne, is stated in the Aberdeen Breviary
to have been assigned to the Vicar of Banchory by
the Abbot of Arbroath, in 1484, with the bell of St.
Ternan. The Airlie Charters record the transference
of land at Lintrathen, in Forfarshire, with the bell

[1] Dr. J. Anderson's "Scotland in Early Christian Times,"
First Series, p. 210.

of St. Medan, from Michael David the bearer of the bell to Sir John Ogilvy. The bells of St. Kessog and St. Lolan were included amongst the feudal investitures of the earldom of Perth, down to 1675. The Brechbennock, a relic of St. Columba, supposed by Dr. J. Anderson to be identical with the Monymusk reliquary, had lands pertaining to it, mentioned in charters of the thirteenth and fourteen century, as being granted with the Brechbennock, by King William, the Lion, to the monks of Aberbrothock, and subsequently by the Abbot of that place to Malcolm of Monymusk, in Aberdeenshire. The practice of swearing on relics was so universal as hardly to require the mention of special examples. The bell of St. Columbkill, in the collection of Mr. John Bell, of Dungannon, was called "Dia dioghaltus," or God's vengeance, in allusion to the curse which was implicitly believed would fall upon any one taking a false oath upon it. The heavy penalty exacted for the profanation of the Bell of St. Patrick's Will, in the year A.D. 1044, has already been referred to, and the Annals record that, in A.D. 1012, the tribe of Conailli were invaded by Maelsechlain in revenge for the violation of St. Patrick's crozier. The method of recovering stolen property by means of a relic was by calling together all the suspected persons and compelling them to clear themselves, by swearing to their innocence of the crime upon it. The Clog-oir, or, Golden Bell of St. Sennan, in the Museum of the Royal Irish Academy, and the Clog-na-fullah, or Bell of Blood, were both employed for this purpose.

As instances of carrying relics with an army to ensure victory, we have the Psalter of St. Columba, called the Cathac (*i.e.*, belonging to battles), which, "if carried three times right round the army of Cinell Chonailli at going to battle, was certain to return victorious"; the crozier of St. Columba, called the "Cath Bhuaidh," and the Brechbennoch, another relic of the same saint, already mentioned as being probably identical with the Monymusk reliquary.

Healing properties were believed to be inherent in the relics of Celtic saints, as in the case of the Black Bell of St. Patrick, which was used to cure rheumatism, by passing it round the body for a fee of two pence enacted by the Gerachty family, living near Ballinrobe, and who were the hereditary keepers. The Bell of Ballynaback, called the Clog Beannighte, was placed near any member of the Henning family, who were its keepers, when dangerously ill, and the "sweating of the bell," caused by the condensation of moisture upon the cold metal in a hot sick-room, was supposed to foretell the death of the patient. Mad persons were at the end of the last century placed in a stone trough in Strathfillan churchyard, Perthshire, with St. Fillan's Bell on their head, and left thus tied down all night in order to effect a cure.

This same bell would, it was believed, return miraculously to its resting-place in the churchyard, if removed by any evilly-disposed person. A similar legend is attached to the Bell of St. Adamnan, preserved in the church at Insch, near Kingussie. Other supernatural powers were possessed by some relics such as the Clog Mogue, or Bell of St. Modoc, which, when placed on a flag-stone, by St. Kilian, floated with St. Modoc across a stream of water in order that he might be baptized. The special privileges and powers attaching to the relics of early Celtic saints were part of that general system of organisation which enabled Christianity to cope successfully with the surrounding paganism. This is put most clearly and graphically in the following passage in Dr. J. Anderson's "Scotland in Early Christian Times"[1] :—"These Christian communities formed, as it were, separate family organisations within the tribe, to which the members were drawn by special advantages, religious, educational, and social, not the least notable of which were a greater degree of security for life and property, and the special protection of the weak against the rapacity and oppression of the strong, which sprang necessarily from the inculcation of the doctrines of the Christian faith. . . . . Acting in obedience to the natural instinct which impels men to seek the greatest security for themselves and their possessions, they were not slow to appreciate the benefit of its tranquillising influences, its right of sanctuary, and its days of rest, its germs of culture and its gospel of peace."

Leaving the history and association of the relics, we will now proceed to describe the objects themselves.

The typical features of the Celtic bell are its quadrangular shape, its small size, and the loop at

[1] First Series, p. 232.

the top, by which it may be easily swung by hand. The bells are of two kinds, as regards the materials of which they are made, those of wrought iron and those of bronze. The iron bells are constructed of a thin plate hammered into the desired shape, and rivetted up the side, like a sheep bell. The loop and tongue are attached in the usual way. The whole is generally coated with bronze to prevent corrosion. The height varies from 9 in. to 18 in., and the average size of the bottom is about 8 in. by 6 in. The bronze bells are cast in one piece, with the handle, which is often ornamented with beasts' heads, where it joins the body of the bell. Examples of this zoomorphic treatment of the handle exist in the bells of St. Fillan, St. Ruadhan, and Langwynodl, in Carnarvonshire. As examples of bronze bells with plain loops, we may take the one at Insch, near Kingussie, and that of St. Finan, at Eilan Finan, in Loch Shiel, Ardnamurchan. The shrines in which many of the bells are incased are composed of metal plates forming a box round it of the same shape as the bell within, including the handle at the top. The outside is decorated with Celtic interlaced filigree work, and sometimes figure subjects. There are about eighty-two Celtic bells, whose existence is at present known, of which fifty-five are in Ireland, fifteen in Scotland, nine in Wales, or in the borders, two in France, and one in Switzerland. The following is a list of bell shrines :—

Bell shrine of Maelbrigde, in the collection of Mr. Robert Day, jun., of Cork, inscribed in minuscules.

Bell shrine of St. Patrick's Will, in the museum of the Royal Irish Academy, inscribed in minuscules ; date A.D. 1091 to 1105.

Bell shrine of St. Culan, in the British Museum.

Bell shrine of St. Mogue.

Bell shrine of St. Mura.

Bell shrine of St. Sennan.

Bell shrine of Connal Gael.

Bell shrine of Kilmichael Glassary, in Museum of Antiquities, in Edinburgh ; style, fourteenth century.

Bell shrine at Guthrie, Forfarshire, inscribed in black letter ; style, fifteenth century.

There are two bronze bells with minuscule inscriptions, one found at Ballynaback, co. Armagh, and the other at Stival, near Pontivy, in Brittany.

The "cumdachs," or book shrines, in which many of the most precious Irish MSS. have been enclosed, are simply rectangular boxes, made to fit the shape and size of the volume, and covered with metal plates, decorated in the usual Celtic fashion. The following list gives the cumdachs which are, or were, once in existence [1] :—

Cumdach of the Book of Durrow, A.D. 877–914.

,,	,,	Armagh, A.D. 938.
,,	,,	Kells, A.D. 1007.
,,	,,	St. Molaise's Gospels, A.D. 1000–1025.
,,	,,	Stowe Missal, A.D. 1023–1064.

[1] Taken from Petrie's "Christian Inscriptions in Ireland," vol. ii. p. 159.

Cumdach of the Book of Columba's Psalter, A.D. 1038–1106.
,,   ,,   Dimma's Book, A.D. 1050–1220.
,,   ,,   St. Patrick's Gospels, 1319–1353.
,,   ,,   Cainnech's Calendar, A.D. 1534.

The croziers of the Celtic church are ornamental metal cases, made to inclose the wooden pastoral crook of some early saint. The straight portion is composed of tubes of sheet bronze riveted up the side, and joined together by bulbous socket-pieces. There is a pointed spike at the bottom, and the crook at the top is bent round into a horse-shoe shape, with a flattened end, instead of coiling round into a spiral, and ornamented along the outer side by a sort of cresting. There are several of these croziers preserved in the museums at Dublin, Edinburgh, London, and in private collections, the following being the most important examples :—

Crozier at Lismore, at Lismore Castle, co. Waterford, inscribed in minuscules ; date A.D. 1090 to 1113.
Crozier of Kells, in the British Museum, inscribed in minuscules ; date A.D. 967 to 1047.
Crozier of St. Dympna, inscribed in minuscules.
Crozier of Clonmacnois, in the Museum of the Royal Irish Academy.
Crozier of St. Fillan, in the Museum of Antiquities in Edinburgh.
Crozier of St. Moluag, belonging to the Duke of Argyll.

The most characteristic form of Celtic reliquary is a quadrangular metal box with sides inclined inwards, and a cover made like the roof of a house. This is the shape given to the Temple at Jerusalem, in the picture of the Temptation of Christ, in the Book of Kells. The following is a list of reliquaries of this class :—

> Shrine of St. Manchan, in the Roman Catholic Chapel of Boher, in the parish of Lemanaghan, King's County.
>
> Reliquary of St. Modoc, in the Museum of the Royal Irish Academy.
>
> Reliquary found in the Shannon, in the Museum of Antiquities, in Edinburgh.
>
> Reliquary in the Museum of the Royal Irish Academy.
>
> Reliquary preserved at Monymusk House, Aberdeenshire.
>
> Reliquary in the Copenhagen Museum, inscribed in Runes, found in Norway.

Another kind of reliquary is made in the shape of the portion of the body of the saint enshrined, as for example, the—

> Shrine of St. Lactin's Arm, in the Museum of the Royal Irish Academy, inscribed in minuscules; date A.D. 1118 to 1127.
>
> Shrine of St. Patrick's Tooth, in the Museum of the Royal Irish Academy, inscribed in Lombardic capitals ; date, *circa* 1376 :—
>
>> "Corp Naomh " (the Holy Body).

The remaining objects belonging to the Celtic Church are the Processional Cross of Cong, the Ardagh Chalice, a bronze altar vessel found at Island Magee, co. Antrim, a bronze plaque with the Crucifixion upon it, found at Athlone ; and the leather covers of the Breac Modog and of the cumdach of the Book of Armagh.

Full descriptions of these objects, and the others mentioned previously, will be found in—

Dr. Petrie's "Ecclesiastical Architecture in Ireland."

Dr. Petrie's "Christian Inscriptions in Ireland."

The Rev. J. Ellacombe's "Bells of the Church."

Dr. J. Anderson's "Scotland in Early Christian Times."

H. O'Neill's "Fine Arts of Ancient Ireland."

Miss Margaret Stokes's "Early Christian Art in Ireland."

"Vetusta Monumenta," vol. vi.

"Archæologia Cambrensis."

"Ulster Journal of Archæology."

"Proceedings of the Society of Antiquaries of London."

"Archæologia."

CHAPTER IV.

EARLY CHRISTIAN ART IN CELTIC MANUSCRIPTS, METALWORK, AND SCULPTURE.

ANY cause, such as religion, which produces a radical change in the ideas of a nation, must necessarily have a powerful effect upon the outward expression of those ideas in art. Religion can create, modify, or destroy the art of a particular country, but can never leave it in the same condition it was previously. Thus, each of the three great religions of the world, Christianity, Mahomedanism, and Buddhism, has its own peculiar style of art, with local variations according to the country in which the new form of belief was implanted.

In the present chapter we propose to confine our inquiry to the modifications in the native art of Great Britain which followed as a direct result of the introduction of Christianity.

The earliest Christian art of which we have any knowledge was engrafted upon the classical art of ancient Italy, and during the first four centuries A.D. was confined almost exclusively to the paintings in the catacombs at Rome.

The chief traces of Roman art in Great Britain have been found on mosaic pavements, sculptured bas-reliefs on tombstones, and portable objects of fictile ware and metal. On some of these Christian symbols appear, but none of the representations of figure subjects are other than Pagan, so that Christianity cannot be said to have influenced the art of this country to any appreciable extent during the period of the Roman occupation, terminating A.D. 410. Shortly after the final departure of the Romans from Britain the Saxon invasions began, and at about the same time the first Christian missionaries landed in Ireland, the result being that England remained Pagan for two centuries whilst a Celtic Church was being firmly established in Ireland, Scotland, and Wales. At the time when the Irish and the other Celts were converted to Christianity at the beginning of the fifth century, classical art had almost entirely died out in Italy, and was rapidly superseded by the Byzantine style, which owed its origin to the removal of the seat of government of the Roman Empire to Constantinople, thus bringing it into more close relationship with the East. The earliest kind of Christian art which was introduced into Great Britain was Byzantine in the first instance, but after being engrafted upon the native Pagan art it became intensely Celtic in character.

Our knowledge of the capacity possessed by the Pagan Celt for art is derived principally from the study of objects of bronze dug up from time to time, and now preserved in public museums in London, Edinburgh, Dublin, Bedford, Liverpool, and Norwich. These objects consist of horse-trappings, helmets, shields, sword-sheaths, mirrors, armlets, and spoon-shaped articles of unknown use. They have been

discovered at various places in England, Scotland,
Wales, and Ireland, and therefore belong to the
period when the Celts occupied the whole of Great
Britain. In some cases, as at Saham Tony, in Norfolk, and Stanhope Farm, Peeblesshire, the objects of
Celtic manufacture have been found associated with
Roman coins, Samian ware, and metal cooking-vessels,
thus giving an approximate date to the style of art
which Mr. A. W. Franks calls "late Celtic."

The most important finds of bronze horse-trappings
have been at Polden Hill, Somersetshire ; Hagbourn
Hill, Berkshire ; Westhall, Suffolk (described in the
Archæologia, vols. xiv., xvi., and xxxvi.) ; at Saham
Tony, Norfolk (Journal of the Norfolk Archæol. Soc.,
vol. ii.), Stanwick and Arras, Yorkshire (York Meeting
of British Archæological Institute). For further infor-
mation on the subject the reader may consult J. M.
Kemble's " Horæ Ferales," Dr. J. Anderson's " Scot-
land in Pagan Times," 1st Series ; "Archæologia
Cambrensis," 4th Series, vol. i. ; "Journal of the
British Archæological Institute," vols. xxvi., xxx. ;
"Archæologia," vols. xxiii., xl. ; " Journal of the
Archæol. Assoc. of Ireland," vol. vi., Series 4 ; Dr. C.
Bruce's " Catalogue of the Alnwick Museum "; and Sir
W. Wilde's "Catalogue of the Royal Irish Academy."

An examination of any large collection of Celtic
bronzes of the Pagan period is sufficient to show that
at about the time of Julius Cæsar's landing in this
country our ancient British ancestors had attained to
extraordinary proficiency in metalwork of all kinds.
The bronze of which their accoutrements, horse
trappings, and personal ornaments were made was

L

brought into the required shape either by casting or by manipulating thin plates with the hammer, the particular process chosen being dictated by the circumstances of the case. The joints were made by riveting, and, as far as construction goes, the Pagan Celts seem to have been quite as skilled as the best workmen of the present day. The decorative features were produced in the form given to the mould when the metal was cast, or by *repoussé* work and chasing when it was wrought. *Champ-levé* enamel was also freely used, generally in small circular plaques fixed on to the rest of the work with a pin. The style of the ornament is so peculiar that a "late Celtic" object may be recognised at a glance. The chief characteristic is the predominance of spiral curves formed by two lines enclosing a space between them which gradually contracts or expands at different points along its length. In the *repoussé* work this space between the two curved boundaries is raised above the surface of the rest, having a moulded section with a sharp ridge in the middle intended to emphasise the path of the curve. The expanding space bounded by two spiral lines often terminates in a trumpet-shaped end, and circular bosses or plaques of enamel mark the starting-points of the volute. Where two trumpet-ends meet an almond-shaped boss is produced. The spaces between the curves are often filled in with hatching composed of short straight lines. This is especially the case on flat surfaces such as the backs of mirrors. It has not yet been ascertained whether this style of ornament originated in Great Britain. The greatest number of

(No. 6.)
Panel of Knotwork formed of double bands on Cross-shaft at Bewcastle.
(From a rubbing by J. R. ALLEN.)
Scale $\frac{1}{6}$ real size.   p. 147.

objects on which it occurs have certainly been found
in this country, but a few have been dug up on the
Continent, so that further researches may perhaps
show that it was invented by some prehistoric people
abroad who may have migrated here. Spiral decoration of "late Celtic" character is not confined
entirely to metalwork, but also occurs on sculptured
stones of the sepulchral chambers at Newgrange, co.
Meath, and Clover Hill, co. Sligo ; and on two knife-
like objects of bone from a chambered cairn at
Slieve-na-Callighe, co. Meath.

The whole of the ornament of the "late Celtic"
style is produced by curved lines, with the exception
of the hatching already mentioned and the patterns
on some of the circular enamelled plaques, examples
of which are to be seen on a shield found in the
River Witham, and on armlets from Pitkellony,
Perthshire, and Castle New, Aberdeenshire. Celtic
art of the Pagan period was of the most abstract kind,
consisting of geometrical ornament only, there being
hardly any attempt to conventionalise animal[1] and
vegetable forms, and none to represent the human
figure.

After the introduction of Christianity, Celtic art,
although retaining the spiral decoration of Pagan
times, received several important modifications, and
had its scope very considerably enlarged by being
applied not only to metalwork, but to sculptured

---

[1] The few specimens of conventionalised animal forms are
a bronze swine's head in the Banff Museum ; a head with horns
at Abbotsford ; and three armlets terminating in a serpent's
head, one of which was found on the Culbin Sands, Elginshire.

stonework and the illumination of the MSS. used in the services of the Church. In the highest kind of art, such as that practised by the ancient Greeks, the representation of the human figure occupies the foremost place, and mere ornament is entirely subordinated to it. Judged by this standard, Celtic Christian art is certainly not the best the world has seen, for quite the reverse is true of it. The Celt excelled in designing the most intricate forms of ornament and executing them with marvellous skill, but his figure-drawing was of almost barbaric rudeness.

Celtic ornament of the Christian period derives its peculiar appearance from a combination of certain purely geometrical elements, consisting of spirals, key-patterns, and interlaced work with conventionalised animals and foliage. The origin of the spirals may be traced to the metalwork of Pagan times, and the germs of the key-patterns and interlaced work may have been introduced into this country with the early MSS. of the Gospels, to be subsequently developed and improved by the Irish illuminators. Some fanciful theorists believe that the interlaced work was copied from the designs on Roman pavements, for-getting that, in Ireland, where it was most largely used, Roman buildings are conspicuous by their absence. Others see a resemblance between the interlaced patterns and basket-work or wattle-work, but such wild guesses are hardly worthy of serious consideration. It is far more probable that this kind of ornament came from the East at the time when Byzantium was the capital of the Roman Empire.

(No. 7.)
Panel of Circular Knotwork on Cross-shaft at Kells.
(From a rubbing by J. R. ALLEN.)
Scale ⅛ real size.

The Nestorian Christians use interlaced work at the present day in the decoration of their MSS., churches, and sepulchral monuments exactly in the same way as the Irish Christians did in the seventh century. The Nestorians, owing to the remoteness of their situation, have thus retained the style of art which was at one time common all over Christendom. Much light may be thrown on the art of ancient Ireland by comparing it with that of other branches of the Eastern Church, such as the Coptic and the Abyssinian. Interlaced work is not by any means confined to Ireland, for it is found on the sculptured stonework of churches in Italy, Dalmatia, Greece, and France, as well as in Saxon, Carlovingian, Lombardic, and Spanish MSS.

Celtic interlaced work, however, differs from all other in the complicated nature of the patterns, the extraordinary fertility of invention exhibited by the designer in producing new variations, and the extreme accuracy with which the drawing is executed.

Interlaced work may be defined as ornament composed of narrow bands or cords following intricate curved paths so as to cover a whole surface, and overlapping each other at regular intervals. In Celtic interlaced work the bands pass under and over alternately with unfailing precision, a mistake in this respect being of the rarest possible occurrence. Interlaced work may be divided into the following classes : (1) that consisting of looped bands ; (2) of twisted bands ; (3) of plaited bands ; and (4) of knotted bands. It would be difficult, without a large number of diagrams, to explain here all the different varieties of each class, and the reader is therefore referred to a paper on the subject by J. Romilly Allen in the "Proceedings of the Society of Antiquaries of Scotland" (vol. xvii. p. 211). The plait-work is often modified by leaving blank spaces at intervals. This is done by cutting off the cords and joining them up to each other all round the blank space instead of letting them run on continuously. In this way knot-work, consisting of one or more cords formed into a knot, which is repeated over and over again, may have been developed. It must be distinctly understood that what are here called knots are not usually ones which could be practically tied in a string, without getting into a hopeless tangle when the ends of the cords are pulled tight. The so-called knots are really only a series of spaces on a flat surface formed by making one or more cords follow a definite path, crossing each other at intervals, so that, if the overlapping were omitted, it would resolve itself simply into a sort of reticulation covering the whole. In the most elaborate kind of Celtic interlaced work the elementary knot, which is repeated over and over again, has two bands crossing at right angles in the centre, and four smaller knots enclosed within bands forming a circle round them. Some of the simpler knot-work patterns are made more complicated by weaving an extra band or two running continuously throughout the whole length. Every band in the interlaced work is eventually joined up to some other, so that loose ends do not occur anywhere. The patterns commence and terminate, in consequence, with a different knot from the one which is repeated throughout its entire length. Where a band changes its direction, it generally turns round with an even circular curve, but in particular places the curve comes to a point like that of a Gothic arch. This is done chiefly to emphasise the sharper curves, and to introduce a certain amount of variety. Interlaced work with square corners is rare in Celtic art, but not uncommon in that of Scandinavia.

Key-patterns are so called from their resemblance to the appearance produced by the slits cut in a key to allow it to pass the wards of the lock into which it fits. The Greek fret is the best known example of this kind of ornament, and other varieties occur in Chinese decorative art. Key-patterns are composed entirely of straight strokes, with others branching out from them, either at different points along the length of the stroke or from the end of it. When a surface is covered in this way the breadth of the space between each stroke should be equal to that of the stroke, so that the background also forms another key-pattern, but of course of a different colour. Key-patterns resemble the labyrinths that are represented on the coins of Gnossus in Crete, and such as were used for devotional purposes in the Middle Ages; for if the black strokes of a key-pattern drawn on a white sheet of paper are supposed to be walls, the space between them will be a passage of uniform breadth throughout, by traversing the total length of which a person might meander over the whole surface covered by the key-pattern, without omitting any portion. The difference of the Celtic key-patterns and others arises from the skeleton plan on which the design is based. All purely geometrical ornament is set out on a surface divided into squares, equilateral triangles, or regular hexagons by lines intersecting at angles of 90°, 60°, or 30°, for reasons it is not necessary to go into here. The pattern is made by filling in the squares, triangles, or hexagons, according to the fancy of the designer, and connecting the isolated parts together so as to form a consistent whole. Finally, the original guiding lines are removed, in order that the artificial nature of the process may not be too apparent. The relation of the border to the setting-out lines plays an important part in the design of ornament. The most characteristic Celtic key-patterns are founded on the square system and the setting-out lines are placed diagonally, cutting the border of the surface to be decorated at an angle of 45°. In this case there are three courses open to the designer :— (1) he can adjust his margin to the pattern, that is to say, make it follow the outline of the squares used for setting out ; (2) he can adjust the pattern to the margin, that is, have a straight margin and fill in the small triangles thus formed all round the edge differently from the rest ; or (3) he can draw the margin quite independently of the pattern, like cutting off a piece of figured wall-paper with a pair of scissors. The first course is seldom resorted to, as it makes the margin crooked ; the second is the one chosen by the Celtic designer, and the third is employed in Chinese art. The peculiarities of the Celtic key-patterns have thus arisen from a desire to make each piece of ornament complete in itself, and from the

(No. 8.)
Panel of Key-pattern on Cross-shaft at St. Andrew's.
(From a rubbing by J. R. ALLEN.)
Scale ⅛ real size.   *p.* 152.

importance given to the border. The lines or strokes
of most of the Celtic key-patterns branch off at angles
of 90° and 45° from each other. When the angle is
as sharp as 45°, the disagreeable effect is taken away
by filling in the corners with little triangles of the
same colour as the strokes. In covering a surface
with a key-pattern it is necessary to have some definite plan of connecting the various strokes together.
One method is to draw a zigzag line following the
sides of the squares used for setting out, and fill in
the squares on each side with frets branching out
from the crooked stem. Another is to cover the
surface with strokes arranged in the form of the letter
H, and join the ends together with frets. In Celtic
ornament the upper half of the left-hand vertical
stroke of the H, and the lower half of the right-hand
vertical stroke, are bent at angles of 45° to the horizontal bar, making a sort of cross between a Z and
an H. This is done in order to adapt the pattern to
the margin, which cuts the squares used for setting out
at an angle of 45°, dividing them diagonally in half.

The spiral ornament of the Christian period bears
a very close resemblance to that found on the Pagan
metalwork, the chief difference between the two
being that in the former the volute is more elaborate
and makes a larger number of turns round the centre,
so that it becomes of greater importance than the
divergent band which connects the volutes together,
whereas in the latter the long sweeping curves of the
connecting band form the principal feature in the
design.[1] The Christian spiral-work consists of a

[1] Miss M. Stokes's " Early Christian Art in Ireland," p. 74.

series of volutes composed of bands coiled together
closely at starting and then running off at a tangent
to join other volutes. The volutes are alternately
right and left-handed, so that the band which
connects the two is C-shaped. The band expands
in the middle of the C so as to form a cusp, and a
small almond-shaped spot is placed across it at this
point. The appearance thus produced is not unlike
two curved trumpets with their mouths placed close
together. Two volutes to be joined are seldom
both right-handed or both left-handed, so that the
connecting band follows an S curve, as is often the
case in the Pagan metalwork. In some of the
volutes the closely-coiled band takes a large number
of turns before it diverges, and the space covered by
its convolutions is approximately circular, but there
are others in which the band only makes about half a
turn before diverging. In the latter the band
becomes broader near the centre of the volute, where
it curls over a little like the top of a Phrygian cap.
The volutes are generally composed of two or more
bands starting from one centre, each volute being
connected with a corresponding number of others
according to how many bands there happen to be.
Spiral patterns can be very easily adapted to fill in
a surface of any shape, for the circular spaces occupied by the close coils of one class of volute can be
increased or decreased in size by altering the number
of convolutions; and in the case of the other kind,
which resembles a Phrygian cap, the curves may be
so adjusted as to bring the centres into any position.
The C-shaped curves which connect the volutes

together are so drawn that their backs touch, leaving a large number of triangular spaces bounded by one concave and two convex arcs of a circle. These triangular spaces form the background, being coloured dark in the MSS. and recessed on sculptured stonework. They are relieved by circular and almond-shaped dots. The centres from which the volutes spring are ornamented in a variety of different ways; sometimes the volute starts from a circular space covered with a large number of smaller volutes, or from three birds' heads. The most wonderful thing about the spiral ornament found in the best MSS., such as the Books of Kells and Lindisfarne, is the unerring precision with which the curves are drawn. Although the bands are sometimes not more than the hundredth part of an inch apart, and make a sufficient number of turns to cover a circle half an inch wide, there is hardly ever an instance of one line running into another, nor did the hand which drew them falter for one moment so as to produce a broken-backed curve. This was the kind of draughtsmanship which commanded the unqualified admiration of Giraldus Cambrensis when he visited Ireland in the twelfth century, and of which Miss Margaret Stokes says:— "No copy of such work as this can convey an idea of the perfection of execution shown in the original; for, as with the skeleton of a leaf, or any microscopic work of nature, the stronger the magnifying power brought to bear upon it, the more is this perfection revealed." Professor I. O. Westwood, although a most skilled draughtsman and master of all the intricacies of Celtic ornament, has had to give up in despair the attempt to trace a whole page from one of the Irish MSS. Spiral ornamentation is charac- teristic of the art of the best period, and the degrada- tion of the style is marked by its disappearance.[1] Volutes occur on the sculptured stones of Ireland and Scotland in the greatest perfection, occasionally on those of the North of England, but hardly ever on those in Wales. In sculptured stonework the central portion of each spiral is, generally raised above the surface so as to form round bosses, the appear- ance of which is very effective. The spiral work on the Pagan metalwork is very irregularly disposed over the surface to be decorated, but during the whole of the Christian period there was a gradual tendency towards a more symmetrical arrangement of the centres of the volutes and towards making the volutes of the same size, until at last the connecting band was reduced to the same breadth throughout and the background with its almond-shaped dots done away with. The spiral work thus developed is in reality a key-pattern, disguised by making the turns round instead of angular.

The conventionalised animal forms made use of in Celtic ornament consist of beasts, birds, and serpents with their bodies, limbs, wings, ears, and tails interlaced in every conceivable manner. Occasionally the human figure is similarly treated, one very favourite device being to place four men so as to form a swastica or

[1] " It is seen in its most perfect development in the illu- minated books of the 7th, 8th, and 9th centuries, but seems to die out after the year 900."—Miss M. Stokes, " Early Christian Art in Ireland," p. 75.

filfot. Most styles of art are, to begin with, purely decorative. In the first stage geometrical patterns alone are employed ; these are gradually transformed into foliageous or into zoomorphic ornament, by introducing the leaves, flowers, and fruit of plants, or the heads, tails, and limbs of animals, thus paving the way for the third or pictorial stage, in which all idea of conventionalism is cast aside and objects are represented naturally. Of course there is no rule without an exception, and some races such as the Eskimos and their prototypes the pre-historic cave men have shown a natural aptitude for figure drawing, unaccompanied by any taste for ornament. Perhaps the necessity of expressing ideas by means of picture writing, which preceded the invention of letters, may explain the reversal of the usual method of development. In Celtic art, at all events, the zoomorphic patterns seem to have been derived from interlaced work. The undulating bands are suggestive of the body of a serpent or the neck of a swan, the only thing required to complete the resemblance being to add a head at the end of the band. The conventionalising thus commenced would soon be applied to other animal forms. The initial letters in the Irish MSS. are almost always made into beasts or birds by the judicious addition of heads, tails, limbs, or wings, and the amount of ingenuity shown in this kind of design is really wonderful. The initials in the Lombardic MSS. are very similar, many of the letters being made out of fish placed in various positions, a peculiarity occurring in the Books of Kells and Armagh. Spirals are retained in the eyes, ears, and junctions of the limbs of the animals with their bodies. Occasionally the bodies of the animals are decorated with interlaced work or key-patterns.

With the exception of the Book of Kells there is no early Irish MS. in which conventionalised plants are to be found. Scrolls of foliage are characteristic of the sculptured stones existing in the portions of Great Britain, formerly covered by the ancient kingdoms of Northumbria, Strathclyde, and the northern half of Mercia. As good examples we may mention the crosses at Bakewell and Eyam, Derbyshire; Ilkley and Sheffield, Yorkshire; Bishop Auckland, county Durham; Bewcastle, Cumberland; Ruthwell, Dumfriesshire; and Abercorn, Linlithgow-shire. In Ireland foliage is not common on the crosses, but it occurs on those at Monasterboice (A.D. 924), county Louth; at Kells, county Meath; and at Clonmacnois, King's County.

The foliage is set out on three different plans—(1) where the stem line is undulating with scrolls in the hollows alternately on the right and left; (2) where the stem line is straight and in the centre of the pattern with scrolls on either side directly opposite each other; and (3) where there are two undulating stem lines forming a twist and interlacing. The centres of the scrolls are generally filled in with fruit conventionally indicated by a series of small round spheres, like a bunch of grapes, the leaves, which are long and pointed, and arranged in groups of three, occupying the spaces on each side. Birds pecking at the fruit, little animals climbing amongst the

(No. 9.)
Circles filled in with Celtic Spiral Ornaments, from the Gospels
of St. Petersburg and of St. Gall.
(Copied from Prof. I. O. Westwood's "Miniatures.")
Scale ¼ real size.   *p.* 154.

(No. 10.)
Panel of Scroll-Foliage and Beasts on Cross-shaft, at Croft.
(From a photograph by J. I'Anson.)

p. 158.

branches and an archer at the bottom shooting upwards at them, are not uncommon features. The foliage described supplies the connecting link between Celtic and Norman art in the same way that the spirals indicate the continuity between Celtic art of the Christian period and that of the Pagan metal-work. The Hiberno-Saxon sculptured stones at Bishop Auckland and Sheffield, with their archers and beasts involved in foliage, may well be compared with the similar designs on the undoubtedly Norman font at Alphington, in Devonshire.

Foliage in Celtic art is therefore an indication of late date, and probably one of the oldest examples is to be seen on the cross of Muiredach, at Monaster-boice (A.D. 924).

The claim of the crosses at Ruthwell and Bew-castle to be of the seventh century must, we think, be abandoned, and of course the same applies to all other monuments which exhibit this style of decoration.

The various peculiarities of the patterns used in Celtic art have now been pointed out, but a great deal of the beauty of the style depends upon the way in which the different elements are combined and arranged. The usual method of procedure was to divide up the surface to be decorated into rectangular panels. Almost every possible way of doing this will be found in the illuminated pages of the MSS. Each panel has a margin of its own, and there is a more prominent one surrounding the whole. In the MSS. the margins are formed of lines of varying thickness and rows of dots; in metalwork they are of twisted or granulated rods; and in sculpture, of roll or cable mouldings. Each panel is filled in with a pattern quite complete in itself, and designed so as to suit the shape of the margin. The kind of pattern chosen to occupy a particular panel was dictated partly with a view to produce a pleasing contrast between the various portions of the design, and partly with a view to make the whole appear symmetrical. Thus the same kind of pattern is never placed in panels next to each other, but in panels situated symmetrically with regard to the centre or the axis of the surface to be decorated. As an example we may take an illuminated page out of the Irish Gospels (No. 51) in the St. Gall Library, Switzerland. The page is rectangular, with a cross of spiral work in the centre and four small oblong panels of interlaced dragonesque animals round it. At the four corners are L-shaped panels of key-patterns, and between them and the rest four T-shaped panels of interlaced work and six small square panels enclosing a step ornament.

We now come to the examples of MSS. metal-work and sculpture executed in the Celtic style.

Manuscripts.

The MSS. with Celtic illuminations are nearly all either copies of the Gospels or the Psalter, written in Latin by Irish scribes. There is no Irish MS. of the Old Testament now extant, and the number of service books besides those already mentioned is very small indeed. The largest collections of Irish MSS. are in the libraries at Trinity College and the Royal

Irish Academy at Dublin, besides which there are many others abroad.[1]

Illustrations of the illuminations will be found in Prof. I. O. Westwood's " Miniatures and Ornaments of the Anglo-Saxon and Irish MSS," the " Palæographical Society Publications," Purton Cooper's "Appendix to Rymer's Fœdera," J. L. Gilbert's "Facsimiles of the National MSS. of Ireland," the Rev. Dr. Reeves on "Early Irish Caligraphy" in the Ulster Journal of Archæology, and Count A. de Bastard's " Peintures et Manuscrits."

The illuminations in the Irish MSS. consist of borders, initials, initial pages, ornamental pages, and miniatures.   The borders are formed of a narrow band of ornament arranged in panels, surrounding the whole page, and enclosed between marginal lines. The size of the initials depends upon the importance of the passage at the commencement of which it is placed.   The initials of the first verse of each of the four Gospels, that beginning the genealogy of Christ in St. Matthew's Gospel, and of the 1st, 51st, and 101st Psalms of the tripartite Psalter generally fill a whole page.   The Latin words with which the four Gospels open are as follows : St. Matthew—Liber generationis ; St. Mark—Initium Evangelii IHV XPI ; St. Luke—Quoniam quidem multum nam sint; St. John—In principio erat verbum ; and the genealogy of Christ in St. Matthew's Gospel with " XPI autem generatio sic erat."   The first letter is of gigantic size, reaching to the full height of the

[1] See Miss M. Stokes, "Early Christian Art in Ireland," and R. Purton Cooper, "Appendix to Report on Rymer's Fœdera."

M

page; the next two or three occupy about half the
height; and the remainder are written smaller in
lines below. The body of the initial letter is margined
and divided into panels filled with ornament, the ends
terminating in animals' heads and spirals. The curved
X of the XPI at the beginning of the genealogy of
Christ in St. Matthew's Gospel perhaps lends itself
better to decorative treatment than any of the other
initials; besides which, being the monogram of
Christ, it received more special attention. There is
a fine example in the St. Gall Gospels, but the most
beautiful of all is in the Book of Kells (see "Vetusta
Monumenta," vol. vi. pl. 43). Miss Margaret Stokes [1]
says of this masterpiece that, in the six preceding,
"there is a gradual increase of splendour, the cul-
minating point of which is reached in this monogram
of Christ, and upon it is lavished, with all the fervent
devotion of the Irish scribe, every variety of design
to be found in Celtic art, so that the name which is
the epitome of his faith, is also the epitome of his
country's art." In addition to the initial page at the
commencement of each Gospel, there were also three
other illuminated pages, one with a picture of the
Evangelist writing his Gospel, a second with his
symbol,—for St. Matthew, a man or an angel; for
St. Mark, a winged lion; for St. Luke, a winged
bull or calf; and for St. John, an eagle; and a third,
containing an ornamented design, the panels of
which form a cross. In some few copies of the
Gospels other miniatures occur. In the Book of
Kells there are the Virgin and Child, Christ seized

[1] "Early Christian Art in Ireland," p. 13.

by the Jews, and the Temptation of Christ ; in the St. Gall Gospels, the Crucifixion and Christ in Glory ; and in the Würzburg Gospels the Crucifixion. The best initial and ornamental pages are in the Gospels of Kells, and Durrow at Dublin ; that of Lindisfarne, in the British Museum ; that of MacDurnan, at Lambeth ; that of MacRegol, at Oxford ; and those in the libraries at Corpus Christi College, Cambridge, at Paris, and at Stockholm.

The Latin words with which the first psalm of each of the three divisions of the tripartite Psalter commences are as follow :—

1st Psalm, Beatus vir.

51st Psalm, Quid gloriaris.

101st Psalm, Dñe exaudi.

The Irish Psalters are smaller than the Gospels, and the initial pages much less elaborate. A miniature is usually placed opposite the initial page of each of the three divisions of the Psalter, the subjects being taken from the life of David, the most common being, David playing on the harp with his four assistants Asaph, Heman, Jeduthun, and Ethan ; David slaying the lion ; and David fighting Goliath. Sometimes in addition to these scenes there is the Crucifixion. The Irish Psalters in the British Museum (Vit. F. xi.), and at St. John's College, Cambridge, have full-page miniatures. The Hiberno-Saxon Psalter in the British Museum (Vespatian A. i.) contains a most beautiful series of small ornamental initials ; seven illuminated sentences extending across the page at the commencement of the 17th, 26th, 38th, 52nd, 68th, 80th, and 97th Psalms ; and a full-page miniature of David playing the harp at the beginning. The Hiberno-Saxon Cassiodorus' Commentary on the Psalms at Durham also contains two pictures of King David. The smaller initial letters in the Irish MSS. are ornamented in various ways by being made into the shape of animals, birds, and serpents, but they are never what the French call "historié," *i.e.*, having the enclosed part of the letter filled in with a small miniature representing a scene from Scripture.

The colours used in the Irish illuminations are very bright, being principally red, blue, yellow, purple, and green. The general effect of a page of one of the MSS. is much the same as that produced by a brilliant flower-bed or a gorgeous Eastern carpet. The interlaced work and key-patterns are often coloured in with alternate patches like checquerwork. Rows of dots, especially red ones, are characteristic of the style.

The drapery of the figures is treated simply as a surface to be decorated, and either covered with interlaced work, key-patterns and spirals, or the folds conventionalised in a most unsightly way by running a margin of a different colour to the rest round the lines of the folds. In many instances the folds are tied up into knots.

In drawing the human face the curves of the mouth, the nose, and the ears are converted into spirals, which gives a very barbaric appearance and entirely destroys its beauty. The figure subjects bear internal evidence of their Byzantine origin in the way that particular scenes are treated, but otherwise it would be difficult to believe that with good models to copy from the Irish illuminator could have produced such monstrosities. The badness of the figure-drawing becomes all the more extraordinary when contrasted with the consummate skill with which the ornamental details are elaborated.

Metalwork.

In the previous chapter, when describing the portable objects of the later Celtic Church, lists were given of the various specimens of Irish and Scotch ecclesiastical metalwork, such as bells, shrines for books and bells, croziers, reliquaries, chalices, altar vessels, processional crosses, &c. The ornament found on Christian Celtic metalwork differs in no way from that employed in the illumination of the MSS. and the sculpture of the crosses, except in its adaptation to the requirements of another material. Dr. J. Anderson is of opinion that Celtic Christian ornament was highly developed in the MSS. before it was applied to metalwork or sculpture. This is a point which is not easy to settle off-hand, but by consulting the chronological table at the end of Miss M. Stokes's "Early Christian Art in Ireland," it will be seen that the earliest dated MSS. containing ornament belong to the seventh century; the earliest dated metalwork with ornament to the eighth; and dated crosses on slabs with ornament to the ninth. One would not expect it to be otherwise, as the necessity for MSS. would occur from the time when Christianity was first introduced, whereas costly metal shrines and elaborately-sculptured crosses would not be thought of until the Church had been established for some centuries and was beginning to accumulate wealth.

Celtic metalwork of the Christian period, although retaining some of the ornamental forms and processes used previously, differs in many respects from the Pagan metalwork. As a natural result of the increased facilities for intercourse with the Continent, which followed the introduction of Christianity into Ireland, new methods of work were imported from abroad and old ones abandoned. A greater variety of metals was used, and the ways of combining them consequently became more numerous. The pacific tendencies of Christianity also led to a change in the class of objects in which the art of the metalworker was displayed. Whilst he was a heathen the decoration of the shield, the helmet, or the sword-sheath claimed his first attention, but after his conversion the Church set before him the nobler task of beautifying the vessels used in the service of God; and most of the centres of learning, like Clonmacnois, had their schools of metalwork and hereditary families of artificers,[1] the names of many of which have been handed down to the present day. The decorative processes employed by the Pagan metalworker were few, being confined to *repoussé* work,

[1] An entry of the end of the eleventh century on one of the blank pages of the Book of Kells records the purchase of half the house of Mac Aeda, cerd, by Congal O'Breslen, for 1 oz. of gold (see "Miscellany of the Irish Archæol. Soc.," vol. i. p. 127). Mac Aeda was the hereditary cerd, or artificer, at Kells, and the name of his descendant, Sitric Mac Aeda, is mentioned in the inscription on the shrine of Columba's Psalter, called the Cathac (see Petrie's "Christian Inscr.," vol. ii. p. 92).

chasing, and *champ-levé* enamelling, and he made everything of bronze.

The Christian artificer, on the other hand, understood how to prepare various other alloys; how to coat one metal with another by bronzing, gilding, and plating; how to produce patterns by means of filigree-work, chainwork, inlaying, niello; the use of several kinds of enamel, and settings of glass, amber, and crystals. The system of arranging all the ornament in panels, which probably originated in the cross pages of the illuminated MSS., belongs essentially to Christian Celtic art, and its application to metalwork creates another distinguishing feature to differentiate it from that of the preceding Pagan period. Another method of treatment, which seems to be peculiar to the Christian metalwork, is that of forming a chequer or other pattern by piercing holes right through a thin plate and then riveting it on the top of another, so that the lower one can be seen through the interstices of the one above. This is specially characteristic of the book shrines, one of the best examples being the cover of the Stowe Missal in the museum of the Royal Irish Academy.

The inscriptions and antiquity of Irish metalwork have been discussed in the previous chapter. We are now chiefly concerned with the quality of the art exhibited in the manufacture of objects intended for the use of the Church. By far the finest specimen of Celtic ecclesiastical metalwork now in existence is the celebrated Ardagh chalice in the museum of the Royal Irish Academy. It was discovered in 1868 in the rath of Reerasta, in the parish of Ardagh, co.

Limerick, and has been described fully by Lord Dunraven, in the "Proceedings of the Royal Irish Academy" (vol. xxiv. p. 433); and by Miss Margaret Stokes in Dr. George Petrie's "Christian Inscriptions in the Irish Language" (vol. ii. p. 123), and in her "Early Christian Art in Ireland," p. 80. Most of the following particulars are derived from these sources. The Ardagh chalice is 7 in. in height; the bowl is 9½ in. in diameter and 4 in. deep; the foot, 6½ in. in diameter. The bowl is hemispherical, slightly curved outwards at the lip, and provided with two handles. It is supported on a low cylindrical stem, resting on a conical foot with a flat rim all round the edge. Five different metals are used in the manufacture of the cup, namely, gold, silver, brass, copper, and lead.[1] The main body of the vessel is of silver, and the ornamental portions of gold. The rim of the cup is of brass, and plates of lead are inserted between the upper and under surfaces of the flat rim round the outer edge of the foot, to give greater stability to the whole. The number of pieces of which the cup is composed amounts to 354 including twenty rivets. The settings are made of three varieties of enamel together with blue glass and amber. The ornament on the outside of the bowl consists of a narrow raised band, running round the whole just below the rim and through the loops of the handles, divided into 12 panels by circular enamelled bosses. The panels are filled in with interlaced work and dragonesque patterns. On each side

[1] The weight of gold is 1 oz. 2 dwts.; silver, 20 oz. 13 dwts.; and bronze, 9 oz.

of the bowl, immediately below this band and midway between the handles, is a circular cross with a
central boss of enamel and four small settings of blue
glass and amber at the ends of the arms of the cross.
The panels are filled in with delicate spirals. The
loops of the handles are ornamented with recessed
panels of interlaced work in the middle and raised
plaques of enamel on each side. The lower part of
the handle, which is fastened to the side of the bowl,
has three enamelled bosses arranged in the form of a
triangle, a central panel and one between each boss,
filled in with interlaced work and four smaller settings
of blue glass. The enamelled bosses are surrounded
by a circular ring, divided into eight segments and set
with amber. The centre of one of the bosses has a
circle of gold grains at the top, pressed into the
enamel whilst in a state of fusion. The stem is
entirely covered with a continuous piece of interlaced work. The collar at the top of the stem abutting against the bottom of the bowl consists of two
concentric rings, the inner one of continuous spiral
work, and the outer one of continuous interlaced
work. The collar at the bottom of the stem abutting
against the foot is divided into six panels filled in
with key-patterns.

The flat outer rim of the foot is divided into eight
panels by raised plaques of enamel. The under-side
of the foot has in the centre a circular crystal boss
surrounded, first, by a ring divided into twelve segments and set with amber; next, a ring of dragonesque
pattern; then one of amber; one of spiral work and
five of enamelled bosses; and, lastly, a ring of inter-

laced work. The flat rim of the foot on the under-side
is divided into eight panels of chainwork, interlaced
work, and key-patterns, by square raised settings of
blue glass with ornamental pieces of wrought silver
beneath.

All the ornament which has now been described is
in relief on the surface of the vessel, the method of
construction being as follows :—A thin plate of silver
is cut out into the shape of the framework surrounding the panels, and hammered from behind so as to
form a raised moulding or margin. The plate is
then fixed on to the body of the vessel by means of
rivets concealed by the enamelled bosses or settings,
and the panels filled in with plaques of filigree work
composed of fine gold-wire on a *repoussé* background.
These plaques appear to have been made separately
and fixed on afterwards with small pins, the heads of
which are disguised by the design. The ornament
made of plaited silver-wire, on the Ardagh chalice,
is very curious. A similarly-plaited chain is attached
to the Tara brooch in the museum of the Royal Irish
Academy, and a piece 6 in. long was found with a
penannular silver brooch of Celtic workmanship at
Croy, Inverness-shire.[1] Miss Margaret Stokes calls
this species of decoration Trichinopoli work. Besides
the ornaments in relief on the Ardagh chalice, there
is an inscription giving the names of the twelve
Apostles, engraved in capital letters on a background
of minute dots, inclosed between margins of double
incised lines running round the bowl. The margin

[1] Dr. J. Anderson's "Scotland in Early Christian Times,"
Second Series, p. 23.

is carried round the handles and circular crosses, where it terminates in beasts' heads and interlaced work. The names of the Apostles occur in the following order, in the genitive case, meaning that the chalice was dedicated in their honour :—

"PETRI + PAVLI + ANDRI + IACOBI
IOANIS + PHILIPI + BATHOLOMEI + THOMAE
MATHEI + IACOBI + TATHEVS + SIMON."

The forms of the letters correspond with those found in the Irish MSS. of the best period, dating from A.D. 700 to 900.[1] The Ardagh chalice has been chosen as a typical specimen of Celtic ecclesiastical metalwork partly because almost every known process is illustrated in its manufacture, and partly in order to show how the practice of distributing ornament in panels was effected in the case of the particular material of which it was made. During the eleventh century there was a gradual falling off in the excellence of the design and execution of the metalwork. The book shrines of St. Molaise's Gospels (A.D. 1001), and of the Stowe Missal (A.D. 1023), afford the latest instances of spiral work. On the shrine of the Bell of St. Patrick's Will (A.D. 1091) it is entirely absent, but the interlaced work is still arranged in panels and has not suffered degradation. In the works of the twelfth century, such as the shrine of St. Lachtin's Arm (A.D. 1106), the cross of Cong (A.D. 1123), and the cover of Dimma's Book (A.D. 1150), the true Celtic characteristics vir-

---

[1] The peculiar form of the letter "A" on the Ardagh chalice occurs also on the slab of Leviut at Camborne, in Cornwall.

tually disappear. The panel arrangement is less marked or given up altogether, and the ornament consists chiefly of a sort of strapwork in which figure of eight curves predominate. Key-patterns are much less common on Celtic Christian metalwork of all periods than in the MSS. and on the sculptured crosses. Figure subjects occur but rarely, as, for instance, the Crucifixion on three bronze plaques, in the museum of the Royal Irish Academy; the symbols of the four Evangelists on the cover of St. Molaise's Gospels; ecclesiastics with bell and crosier, and a figure playing the harp, on the cover of the Stowe Missal; five groups of figures holding various insignia of office on the shrine of St. Moedog.

A great number of penannular brooches with Celtic ornament upon them have been found at different times in Ireland and Scotland, but as they are not necessarily ecclesiastical we are not concerned with them here. The Tara brooch in the museum of the Royal Irish Academy is one of the best instances; those found in Scotland are described in Dr. J. Anderson's "Scotland in Early Christian Times" (Second Series, Lecture 1). The high estimation in which Celtic art metalwork was held abroad is proved by the number of objects that have been dug up in Norway.[1]

Sculpture

The sculptured stones of Ireland, Scotland, Wales, and the north of England afford a far better means

[1] Hans Hildebrand's "Industrial Arts of Scandinavia," S. K. Handbook, p. 85; Anderson's "Scotland in Early Christian Times," Second Series, p. 29.

for arriving at definite conclusions with regard to the development of Celtic art than either the MSS. or the metalwork, because owing to their less perishable nature the number of specimens which have survived is far greater, and not being easily removed, the monuments remain in their original positions. Our knowledge of Celtic art in Scotland is derived almost exclusively from metalwork and sculpture, but chiefly, from the latter, for the examples of metalwork are rare, and the " Book of Deer," now in the University Library at Cambridge, is the only MS. of the pre-Norman period known to have been written in that country. The method of treating scenes from the Old Testament history can only be studied from the monuments, for there is no MS. copy of this portion of the Bible with Celtic pictures now in existence.

Notwithstanding this, no attempt has yet been made to take casts, photographs, or otherwise illustrate the sculptured stones of the pre-Norman period in Great Britain as a whole; but until such a work is undertaken it is hopeless to form any theories on the subject that will bear the test of time. The value of the early Irish MSS. is so fully appreciated that they have been all secured for our public libraries; the metal shrines, croziers, and bells are treasures beyond the reach of any private collector; but the sculptured stones are allowed to decay from exposure to the weather, or even to be mutilated by persons who are too ignorant or too naturally vicious to understand the harm they are doing.

The area over which monuments exhibiting the peculiar Celtic forms of ornament are spread embraces almost the whole of Great Britain, but they are more thickly distributed in some districts than others, and the quality of the art varies according to the locality. The most difficult point to settle with regard to the origin of Celtic ornament is whether the style was invented in Ireland, and subsequently introduced into other parts of Europe by the Irish scribes, or whether the style existed in a debased form all over Europe, and was simply more highly developed in Ireland than elsewhere. However this may be, the finest specimens of sculptured stonework are to be found in Ireland, consisting of about 250 sepulchral slabs and 45 high crosses. None of these are of earlier date than the ninth century, and if the first supposition as to the origin of the style be true the monuments with Celtic ornament in other parts of Great Britain must have been erected later still.

A careful examination of the series of inscribed slabs at Clonmacnois whose age is known shows very clearly the period at which ornament first begins to make its appearance. The four dated slabs of the seventh century, and the six dated slabs of the eighth century, given in the Chronological List at the beginning of Dr. Petrie's "Christian Inscriptions in the Irish Language" (vol. i. p. 12), have nothing but plain crosses and inscriptions. The first instance of the occurrence of any ornament is on the tombstone of Tuathgal, seventh abbot of Clonmacnois, who died A.D. 806. In the ninth century there are five dated slabs with ornament, in the tenth century ten, in the eleventh century eight, and in the twelfth century only two.

Ornament is very sparingly used on the sepulchral slabs in Ireland, and figure sculpture does not occur at all. As typical examples of decorated slabs we may take that of St. Berecthir (A.D. 839) at Tullylease, co. Cork, and those of Conaing, Lord of Teffia (A.D. 821) ; Suibine Mac Maelhuma, scribe of Clonmacnois (A.D. 887) ; Maeltuile, lector of Clonmacnois (A.D. 921) ; and St. Fiachra (A.D. 921), at Clonmacnois.

The sculpture on the high crosses is of a far more elaborate character than that on the sepulchral slabs, and it is also cut in greater relief. In Ireland there are thirty or more of these profusely-decorated crosses, the dates of six of which have been ascertained by means of the names mentioned in the inscriptions upon them, varying from the tenth to the twelfth century. The most interesting and perfect examples are at Clonmacnois, King's County ; Monasterboice, Louth ; and Kells, co. Meath. A large number of others will be found illustrated in H. O'Neill's work on the subject. The highest point of excellence in sculpture seems to have been attained about the beginning of the tenth century, after which there was a gradual decline in the quality of the art until in the twelfth century the typically Celtic features disappear entirely. The cross at Tuam, co. Galway, erected in A.D. 1123 for Turlogh O'Conor, is one of the latest monuments in which any trace of Celtic feeling can be detected. As an instance of a cross erected when the style was at its best we may take the cross of Muiredach at Monasterboice (A.D. 924). The total height of the monument is 19 ft. The base, or socket stone, is a rectangular truncated pyramid, 2 ft. 3 in. high, in which is fixed a shaft, of rectangular section, 6 ft. 6 in. high. The four arms of the cross are connected by a circular ring, and the hollows in the angles pierced right through. The top arm of the cross is made with a sloping roof like that of the metal shrines and oratories of the period. The whole of the sculpture is arranged in rectangular panels surrounded by a cable moulding, within the roll moulding which forms the angles of the cross. The sides are decorated with ornamental patterns only, but the front and back are entirely covered with figure subjects. The ornament is the same class as that found in the Hiberno-Saxon MSS., consisting of spirals, interlaced work, key-patterns, and dragonesque devices. The figure subjects are evidently intended to teach the people the most vital doctrines of Christianity, by placing before them·a regular series of scenes from Scripture history, all of which foreshadow and lead up to the death of the Saviour of mankind upon the Cross, followed by His second coming to judge the world. Thus on the front of the cross of Muiredach in the centre of the head is placed the Crucifixion, and on the back, occupying a similar position, is the Last Judgment. The subordinate scenes which lead up to the principal ones, as far as they have been yet made out, are the Temptation of Adam and Eve and their expulsion from the Garden of Eden, the Adoration of the Magi, Christ seized by the Jews, Pilate washing his hands, and the Dextera Dei. The subjects on the base do not appear to be Scriptural. They are very much weathered, but a horseman, a Satyr, and a Sagittarius can be detected.

The scheme of the symbolic decoration of most of the Irish crosses is similar to that just described. The principal subjects are always the Crucifixion on one face and the Last Judgment or Christ in Glory on the other; but the subjects on the panels of the shafts vary a good deal, the following being those which occur with the greatest frequency :—

Temptation of Adam and Eve.
Noah in the Ark.
Sacrifice of Isaac.
David and the Lion.
David and Goliath.
David playing the Harp.
Three Children in the Fiery Furnace.
Daniel in the Lions' Den.
Flight into Egypt.
Baptism of Christ.
Miracle of the Loaves and Fishes.
Soldiers guarding the Sepulchre.

From the way in which the different subjects are treated it is clear that the designers of these crosses, or their predecessors, must have had Byzantine models to copy from; and that they must, at all events to a limited extent, have been acquainted with some such system of Christian iconography as that laid down in the Greek Painters' Guide from Mount Athos,[1] which sets forth the ideas of the Eastern Church on the symbolic method of dealing with the

[1] See "Didron's Christian Iconography," edited by Miss M. Stokes.

N

events recorded in the Old and New Testament, so as to connect them together by means of types and antitypes into one great Christian drama, having a single plot running through the whole.

The art of the pre-Norman sculptured stones of Scotland was largely influenced by that of Ireland, and it is consequently very Celtic in character. On the west coast, as at Iona and Kildalton, we get free standing crosses, hardly differing at all from those of Ireland, but the typical form of Christian monument in Scotland is found in the eastern counties, more especially in Perthshire and Forfarshire. It consists of an upright slab with the cross carved in relief upon it, instead of the stone itself being cut out into the shape of a cross. The ornamental patterns are the same as those on the Irish crosses, but they are smaller as regards the scale on which they are executed, and so present a more delicate appearance. As a general rule, the Scotch sculpture is in much lower relief than the Irish. The general effect of the best of the Scotch stones is not unlike that produced by one of the highly-decorated pages at the beginning of the Hiberno-Saxon MSS. of the Gospels. This is due to the shape of the stone, the minuteness of the ornament, and the practice of placing a frame of interlaced work and key-patterns round the edge of the slab, as is done on the crosses at Nigg, Rossie Priory, and Hilton of Cadboll, instead of a roll or cable moulding only. The Scotch crosses are distinguished from those in other parts of Great Britain by the occurrence upon them of certain symbols of unknown meaning, and representations of warriors and hunters on horseback, drawn in a most spirited manner. Illustrations of nearly all the known specimens are to be found in Dr. J. Stuart's "Sculptured Stones of Scotland," and their peculiarities are described in a masterly way by Dr. J. Anderson in his "Scotland in Early Christian Times" (second series). The art of the pre-Norman crosses in Wales is inferior to that of either the Irish or Scotch sculptured stones. The two most common forms of cross in Wales are (1) a cross with a short stumpy shaft and a circular head, like the one at Margam, in Glamorganshire; or (2) a cross with a tall slender shaft and a head like the Irish crosses, but much smaller, like the one at Carew, in Pembrokeshire. The ornament consists chiefly of interlaced work, key-patterns occurring less frequently, and spirals hardly ever. Figure sculpture is uncommon and very rudely executed. Illustrations of the Welsh crosses are given in Professor I. O. Westwood's "Lapidarium Walliæ."

A few crosses with Celtic ornament are to be found in Cornwall, but the art is exceedingly poor as compared even with those of Wales. Illustrations will be found in Blight's "Cornish Crosses," and in a Paper by A. G. Langdon, in the "Journal of the British Archæological Association," vol. xliv. p. 301.

CHAPTER V.

THE ARCHÆOLOGY OF THE SAXON CHURCH
(A.D. 600 TO 1066).

Structures.

WHEN Edward the Confessor rebuilt the Abbey Church of St. Peter at Westminster in A.D. 1065, the style of architecture which he adopted was an entirely new one, introduced into this country from Normandy, and Matthew Paris tells us that the example thus set was followed afterwards in the construction of many other churches. Dr. E. A. Freeman is justly moved to anger by the foreign predilections of King Edward, whom he calls "half a Frenchman"; and it must have been specially galling to Englishmen that during his reign Robert, a foreigner, should have been appointed to the see of Canterbury for the first time since the mission of St. Augustine, when such a man as Ælfric was available for the post. However much we may regret Edward's un-English tendencies in most respects, it was a distinct advantage that the comparatively rude methods of building employed by the Saxons should be improved. Very little now remains of Edward the Confessor's work in Westminster Abbey, but there is enough to prove that the new style referred to by Matthew Paris and

William of Malmesbury was what is now called Norman, and of which we have a fine specimen, erected only a few years later, in St. John's Chapel in the Tower of London. The only inference that can be drawn from the fact of the Norman style of architecture being called a new one, is that there was already existing in England a Saxon style which differed from it. The progress of Gothic architecture in this country after the Conquest is well known to have passed through several advancing stages of development, as attested by a continuous series of dated examples, until it finally died out in the time of the Reformation ; but there are a large number of buildings exhibiting characteristics which are neither Roman nor belonging to the debased classical style of the Renaissance, nor to any of the recognised phases of Gothic, and are therefore, with much reason, classed as being of Saxon origin.

We have seen in a previous chapter that the peculiarities of early Irish architecture resulted from engrafting the Romanesque style of Lombardy upon the native Celtic methods of building in stone. In England the same style was localised and modified by combination with the Saxon methods of building in wood, and the Roman methods of building in brick. The turned balusters and narrow projecting pilasters in some of the Saxon churches suggest the idea of having been designed by a carpenter rather than a stonemason, and the round brick arches in others are directly copied from Roman work. A great number of the Saxon churches must have been of wood, but this material is so perishable by fire

and other causes that only one specimen now remains, which has not been either destroyed or
replaced by a more permanent structure. We have,
then, three distinct types of Saxon ecclesiastical
buildings :—

(1) Churches modelled on the Roman basilica
with arches turned in Roman brick; (2) stone
churches with architectural details, some of which
resemble those found in the early Romanesque
buildings of Lombardy and Germany, and others,
apparently, in imitation of timberwork; and (3)
wooden churches, having more in common with the
buildings in Norway and Sweden than with any
structures now existing in this country.

All Saints', Brixworth, Northamptonshire, may be
taken as the best typical example of a Saxon church
most nearly approximating to the Roman pattern.
The ground-plan of the original building consisted
of a nave 60 ft. long by 30 ft. wide inside with aisles
on both sides, a chancel 30 ft. square with an apsidal
end having a crypt below of similar shape. To this
was subsequently added, but still in pre-Norman
times, a western tower and a circular stair turret.
There is thus Saxon work of two periods, making it
rather difficult to ascertain how much belongs to the
first church. The nave arcades consisted of four
arches on each side turned in Roman brick, opening
into side aisles or a series of small chambers. These
arches are now built up so as to form the side walls
of the nave of the modern church, the aisles having
been destroyed, probably in the fourteenth century.
The plan of the aisles has been made out by

examining the foundations which still remain outside the walls of the modern church. In addition to the nave, chancel aisles, and tower, there are four chambers, two at the east end of the aisles with small doorways leading into the chancel, and two at the west end of the aisles with doorways leading into the tower. Above the nave arcade there is a clerestory with three windows on each side having round-arched heads turned in Roman brick. The chancel also had a clerestory. These features have been supposed by some to form part of the later Saxon additions, but Sir Gilbert Scott expresses considerable doubt on the point. The apse was surrounded by a circular vaulted passage with doorways at each end opening into the chancel. The chancel is divided from the nave by three round arches turned in Roman brick springing from rectangular piers. The arches are of unequal span, the centre one being larger than those at each side. This chancel arch bears a great resemblance to the one at Reculver, described in a previous chapter. The openings in the wall between the nave and the tower consist of two single round-headed apertures, one above the other, and a triple window with two stone balusters, all the arches being turned in Roman bricks. The walls of Brixworth Church are built of oolite mixed with Roman bricks, granite, sandstone, and slate, the masonry being rudely-constructed rubble-work, with herring-bone work in irregular patches. The arches throughout are semicircular, being composed of two courses of brick on edge with a course of bricks laid flat between each and round the outside. The Roman materials were obtained from the ruins of a station near the site of the church.

We have it on the authority of Hugo, a monk of Peterborough, quoted by Leland, that Saxulphus founded a monastery at Brixworth (*circa* A.D. 700).

Another very fine church of the same type as the one at Brixworth, but cruciform in plan, is to be seen on the Castle Hill at Dover. The tower of Trinity Church at Colchester also belongs to the same class.

One of the most perfect examples of a Saxon Church of dressed stone is at Bradford-on-Avon, in Wiltshire, dedicated to St. Lawrence. The ground-plan consists of a nave, 25 ft. 2 in. long, by 13 ft. 2 in. wide inside ; a chancel, 13 ft. 2 in. long by 10 ft. wide ; and a porch on the north side, 10 ft. 5 in. long by 9 ft. 11 in. wide. The foundations of a chamber on the south side corresponding to the porch on the north have been discovered, showing that the plan was originally cruciform. The chancel arch is semicircular with square projecting mouldings springing from a very rude impost. The breadth between the jambs is only 3 ft. 5 in., and on each side are narrow projecting pilasters. The north doorway of the nave is 2 ft. 10 in. wide, and 8 ft. 6 in. high. The architectural treatment of the chancel arch and the doorways is the same. There are three round-headed windows splayed inside and outside ; one in the south wall of the nave, one in the south wall of the chancel, and one in the west wall of the porch. The wall of

the nave is 25 ft. 5 in. high, that of the chancel
18 ft. 4 in., and that of the porch 15 ft. 6 in.

The walls are built of neatly-dressed stone, laid in
regular courses.

The elevation of each side of the building is
divided into three stages : the first, between the
plinth and a string-course above the level of the tops
of the windows, is relieved by narrow projecting
pilasters placed at intervals ; the second is decorated
with arcading running round the whole church just
below the eaves of the roof of the chancel ; and the
third left plain. The gables are ornamented with
narrow, vertical projecting moulded strips of stone.

Two slabs with sculptured angels are built into the
west wall of the nave above the chancel arch. A
monastery was founded at Bradford-on-Avon by St.
Aldhelm, Bishop of Sherborne, at the end of the
seventh century, and William of Malmesbury, writing
four hundred years later, speaks of his " ecclesiola "
as being still in existence, but whether the present
Church of St. Lawrence can be referred to so early
a period seems rather doubtful.

The only wooden church in this country which has
any claim to be of Saxon date is at Greenstead, near
Ongar, in Essex. The building has a nave and
chancel, a porch on the south side, and a western
tower. The most ancient portion is the nave, the
rest being comparatively modern. It measures
29 ft. 9 in. long by 14 ft. wide internally. The north
and south walls are formed of solid oak-tree trunks
placed vertically side by side. Each timber is adzed
flat on the two edges, where it fits against the next

upright and also on the inner face, but the outside is left with the natural round shape of the trunk untouched. The upright timbers are tongued and grooved together, and cut into a wedge-shape at the top so as to fit into a deep V-shaped groove in a horizontal plate, to which each timber is pinned with an oak treenail. In the year 1848 the bottoms of the timbers were found to be so decayed and worm-eaten that the ends had to be cut off, and they are now mortised into a wooden sill supported on a low brick wall. There are twenty-five upright timbers on the north side of the church and twenty-four on the south, 5 ft. 6 in. high up to the plate at the top. The east gable-wall of the nave was removéd when the chancel was built in the sixteenth century, and the west gable-wall is composed of a double layer of planks fastened together with treenails. The only opening in the walls is the south doorway. The nave is lighted from above by dormer windows in the roof, which is modern. A local tradition associates Greenstead with St. Edmund, king and martyr, who was killed by the Danes on the 20th of November, A.D. 870. His body was buried at Eglesdene, and after remaining there for thirty-three years was removed to Bury St. Edmunds. In the year A.D. 1010, in consequence of the ravages of the Danes, the body was taken to London for greater safety, but three years afterwards it was again sent back to Bury St. Edmunds, and on the return journey the bones of the martyr are traditionally believed to have rested in the little wooden chapel at Greenstead, which is on the road from London into Suffolk.

Having now described the three principal types of Saxon churches, we will proceed to examine the various characteristic features of the style. The period during which Saxon Christian buildings were erected in England extends over the 470 years from the landing of St. Augustine on the shores of Kent (A.D. 596) to the Norman Conquest (A.D. 1066), being almost exactly equal to that between A.D. 1066 and the suppression of the monasteries by Henry VIII. (A.D. 1538). The latter period embraces the whole range of Gothic architecture from the massive Norman of St. John's Chapel, in the Tower of London, to the scientifically refined Perpendicular of the fan-vaulting of King's College Chapel, at Cambridge, with all the intermediate stages of Transitional Norman, Early Pointed, Decorated and Flamboyant. No such rapid advances in style are, however, to be detected during the 470 years before the Conquest, and there are so few Saxon churches in complete preservation whose age has been satisfactorily ascertained, that it is almost impossible to trace the development of the style by arranging a series of structures in chronological sequence, so as to compare their various peculiarities. Before the days of Rickman the term Saxon was applied to the round-arched style we now know to be of Norman origin. Since then the existence of a Saxon style distinct from Norman has been entirely doubted by the more sceptical, and others, like the late Sir J. H. Parker, of Oxford, would have us believe that none of the so-called Saxon churches are older than the eleventh century.

The views expressed by Sir Gilbert Scott in his "Lectures on Architecture," and by Dr. E. A. Freeman in his "History of Architecture," will, however, commend themselves to the more rationally-minded amongst us. The latter authority divides the Saxon style into three divisons :—

(1) The direct but rude imitations of Roman work, of which Brixworth is an instance.

(2) The developed Saxon manner, with its high towers, its pilastered strips, and suggestion of imitation of timber-work, as at Earl's Barton.

(3) That in which Norman features are introduced or anticipated.

There is ample historical evidence to show that the Saxons built stone churches at a very early period. The Venerable Bede specifically mentions stone churches in the following passages in his "Ecclesiastical History" :—

(Book iii. ch. 4.) St. Ninian builds a stone church, dedicated to St. Martin, at a place called "Ad Candidam Casam," now Whitherne or Whithorn, in Wigtonshire (A.D. 412).

(Book ii. ch. 14.) King Ædwin of Northumbria, replaces a wooden church at York, dedicated to St. Peter, by one of stone, which is completed by his son Oswald, who succeeded him A.D. 633.

(Book ii. ch. 16.) Paulinus builds a stone church "of remarkable workmanship" at Lincoln (A.D. 627).

(Book iii. ch. 23.) A church of stone is built at Lastingham, in Yorkshire, dedicated to the blessed Mother of God, and Cedd is buried in it to the right of the altar (A.D. 648).

(Book v. ch. 21.) Abbot Ceolfrid of Wearmouth and Jarrow sends architects to Naiton, king of the Picts, to build a church of stone "according to the fashion of the Romans" (A.D. 710).

Also in Bede's "Lives of the Holy Abbots," Benedict Biscop brings back masons with him from Gaul to build the church at Monkwearmouth "in the Roman style, which he always admired" (A.D. 674).

Eddius, in his "Life of St. Wilfrid," written *circa* A.D. 710, tells us in chap. xvi. that the Basilica at Ripon was built of wrought stone from top to bottom, and provided with divers pillars and porticoes (A.D. 661); and in chap. xxii. that at Hexham a more magnificent minster still was erected (A.D. 674), dedicated to St. Andrew, the like of which did not exist on this side of the Alps. Richard of Hexham, writing *circa* A.D. 1138, adds in chap. ii. that the columns and the arch of the sanctuary were decorated with histories and various figures sculptured in relief upon the stone, and with a pleasing variety of painting and colour. Eddius ("Vita Wilfredi," chap. xiv.) says that Wilfrid, when performing the office of bishop in many places in England, took about with him a band of masons ("cæmentarii").

We hear of the stone basilica built by King Cnut, at Ashenden, in Berkshire (A.D. 1017), from William of Malmesbury, and of the Church of St. Michael at St. Albans, constructed of Roman materials from Verulam, in the writings of Matthew Paris.[1]

[1] See "Publications of the Surtees Society," vols. xliv.–xlvi.; "The Priory Church of Hexham and its Chronicles," by J. Raine;

Ground Plan.

None of the cathedrals of the Saxon period are now in existence, and only a few of the churches are sufficiently perfect to enable the ground-plan to be made out. At Escombe, in the county of Durham, at Deerhurst Chapel, Gloucestershire, and at Corhampton, in Hampshire, the plan consists of a simple nave and chancel; at Worth, in Sussex, the church is cruciform, with a circular apse at the east end; the church on the Castle Hill at Dover is cruciform with a central tower. Side aisles are very exceptional, although there are instances at Brixworth, in Northamptonshire, and at St. Michael's, at St. Albans.

Masonry.

The chief peculiarities of the masonry on the exterior of a Saxon church are the pilasters on the face of the walls and the "long and short work" of the quoins. The pilasters are narrow, vertical strips, or flat ribs of stone projecting from the wall. This form of decoration may have been suggested, in the first instance, by timber work; but the chief function of the pilaster seems to be to relieve the monotony of the large flat surfaces produced by the great height of the walls and the smallness of the windows. What

vol. lxxiv., "Memorials of the Church of SS. Peter and Wilfrid, Ripon," by J. T. Fowler ; "Public Record Office Publications"; "Willelmi Malmesbiriensis Monachi De Gestis Regum Anglorum," by Dr. W. Stubbs, vol. i. page 220 ; " Matthæi Parisiensis Monachi Sancti Albani Chron."; "Caxton Soc. Publications " ; and "Rerum Brit. Medii Aevi Script." : " Vita S. Wilfredi," by Eddius.

is technically called "long and short work" consists
in placing the long, narrow quoin stones with the
longest dimension alternately horizontal and vertical.
The quoins and pilasters are always of dressed stone,
the rest of the wall being generally of rubble masonry.
The quoins are in many cases made to project like
the pilasters.   Dr. E. A. Freeman points out that the
narrow Saxon pilasters correspond to the shafts used
for purposes of external decoration in other styles.
The pilasters on the gables at Bradford-on-Avon,
Wiltshire, are moulded, and on the tower at Sompting,
Sussex, the place of the pilaster is taken by a shaft
with capitals running up the middle of the wall.
Sometimes herring-bone masonry occurs in Saxon
churches, as at Diddlebury, Shropshire.

Towers.

All the most characteristic features of Saxon architecture are found in their highest perfection in the
towers of the churches.   Perhaps the best example is
at Earl's Barton, in Northamptonshire.   It is a huge
square mass, without either buttresses or external
stair turret, divided into four stages by plain horizontal
string-courses.   The quoins are of "long and short"
work, and the three lower stories are ornamented on
each side with five narrow projecting pilasters running
vertically upwards.   There is a sort of arcading just
above the first string-course, formed of arches in the
blank spaces between the pilasters, and above the
second string-course there are strips of projecting
stone placed diagonally like the letter X between
each pilaster, resembling the cross bars of timber

construction. The greater part of the top story is occupied by a five-light belfry window, with small, semi-circular heads and turned balusters bellying out in the middle. The vacant space between the window and the angle of the tower is filled in with a vertical pilaster resting on two diagonal strips. The intersections of all the diagonal strips and their points of junction with the vertical pilasters are emphasised by means of square projecting blocks of stone. There is a roundheaded doorway in the lower stage of the tower on the west side and double windows on the south and west sides, with crosses carved in relief on the lintels. There are round-headed windows on three sides of the second stage and triangular-headed ones on three sides of the third stage. The tower at Earl's Barton partakes of the stern qualities of our Anglo-Saxon forefathers, and reminds us of their virtues and their defects. It impresses the beholder by sheer force of its mass, and what is lacking in the refinement of its architectural details is made up for by uncompromising strength of the general design and the archaic appearance of the whole. Other towers very similar to the one at Earl's Barton are to be seen at Barton-upon-Humber, in Lincolnshire, and Barnack, in Northamptonshire.

There is only one Saxon tower now remaining in England which preserves its original top, at Sompting, in Sussex. The roof is of a kind very common on the Rhine, but practically unknown in this country, consisting of a four-sided pyramid placed so that the angles come in the middle of each face of the tower, which has a pointed gable, the four sides of the roof being of a diamond shape. The most common finish was, however, probably a pyramidal roof of the ordinary type.

Belfry Windows.

Before leaving the towers a very curious peculiarity of some of the upper belfry windows must be noticed as being evidently derived from the Lombardic Romanesque style.[1] The windows referred to are double, with semi-circular heads, and a central column, or baluster, placed not flush with the outside face of the wall, as in Norman architecture, but recessed far back, so that the capital supporting the arches becomes a projecting bracket. Examples of this peculiarity occur in the towers at St. Benet's, Cambridge; Sompting, Sussex; St. Mary Bishophill, Junior, York; Hornby, Yorkshire; Wyckham, Berkshire; Waithe, Holton-le-Clay, Clee and Glentworth, Lincolnshire; Northleigh, Oxfordshire; Monkwearmouth, Bolam, and Billingham, Durham; St. Andrew's, Bywell, and Ovingham, Northumberland; and elsewhere. The belfry windows in the towers at Brixworth and at Earl's Barton, Northamptonshire, are exceptional, as there are more than two lights, and the balusters are not recessed back from the face of the wall.

Windows.

The ordinary windows in Saxon churches are of small dimensions, and the height seldom exceeds

[1] See clerestory of the Duomo at Modena, illustrated in Dr. E. A. Freeman's "Historical and Architectural Sketches," p. 250.

O

twice the breadth, so that they have more in common
with the windows in the Irish oratories than with
the long, narrow slits seen in Norman buildings.
Windows of this class exist at Monkwearmouth,
Jarrow, and Escomb, county Durham; St. Andrew's
Bywell, and Ovingham, Northumberland; Boarhunt,
Hants; Comersfield, Buckinghamshire; Wickham,
Berkshire; Diddlebury, Shropshire; Bradford-on-
Avon, Wilts. The window is often placed almost in
the centre of the wall, with deep splays both internally and externally, having the appearance of an eye
set far back in its socket, and the jambs are generally
inclined.

In the towers at Deerhurst, Gloucestershire;
Barton-on-Humber, Lincolnshire; Sompting, Sussex;
and Herring-fleet, Suffolk, there are fine specimens
of double-light windows with triangular heads. The
windows in the north wall of the nave of Escomb
Church, county Durham, are flat headed.

Doorways, Chancel, and Tower Arches.

Most of the doorways in Saxon churches have
round tops, but they are sometimes triangular, as at
Brigstock, Northamptonshire, and Deerhurst, Gloucestershire. The chancel and tower arches are in all
cases round-headed, and treated in the same fashion
as the doorways. The arches are cut square through
the wall, and never broken up into different orders of
mouldings recessed one behind the other, nor are the
jambs stepped and filled in with nook-shafts, as in
Norman architecture. The distinguishing feature of
he Saxon doorways, chancel, and tower arches, is

that the mouldings are placed in relief upon the surface of the wall instead of being cut into it, and the whole opening is surrounded by a sort of frame of rib-work, forming a hood round the top, which is continued down each side of the jambs. The arch is separated from the jamb by an impost of square section, and sometimes the surrounding frame of rib-work has a square overlapping blocks of stone to mark the springing of the arch, and others at the ground level on each side of the jamb. Good specimens of Saxon round-headed doorways remain at Earl's Barton and Wittering, Northamptonshire; Barton - upon-Humber, Lincolnshire; Stanton Lacy, Shropshire; chancel arches at Worth, Sussex; Corhampton, Hampshire; Escomb, Durham; Daglingworth and Deerhurst, Gloucestershire; and tower arches at St. Benet's, Cambridge; Barnack and Brigstock, Northamptonshire. Some of the chancel arches are very narrow; that at Bradford-on-Avon being only 3 ft. 5 in. across between the jambs; at Escomb, 5 ft.; and at Deerhurst Chapel, 6 ft. 4 in. Many of the doorways and other openings in Saxon buildings have no architectural features whatever, the arches being turned in Roman brick, as at Brixworth, Northamptonshire. Sometimes a plain arch springs from an abacus consisting of a square block of stone, but whenever the hood-moulding appears it is carried down to the ground on each side.

Mouldings.

In Saxon buildings architectural effect is obtained almost entirely by the use of narrow projecting ribs of stone of square section. When vertical they take the place of shafts, when horizontal they serve for string-courses, and when round an arch they perform the function of a hood-moulding. The terminations of these ribs consist of square blocks a little wider than the rib, and projecting further from the wall. When there is more than one block they are made to overlap each other. Thus, where in Gothic architecture we should find a carved capital, or a moulded base, in Saxon buildings there is nothing better than a stepping formed of square blocks. The Saxon designers were anything but skilled in the use of mouldings to enhance the beauty of their work, and most of their attempts in this direction are very rude. The Normans developed their arch-mouldings by cutting a roll or a chamfer on the angles of the square stones of the arch, but the Saxons placed the moulding in relief either on the face or the soffit of the arch. In one case the moulding is made by taking away from the original volume of the square stones, and in the other by adding to it. The Saxon mouldings are generally composed of rolls of semi-circular section placed on the face of the stone, not on the angle, combined with V-shaped channellings or square steppings. Good instances of arch-mouldings occur on the doorway of the tower at Earl's Barton and on the chancel arch at Sompting ; of moulded imposts on the tower arches at Barnack, St. Benet's, Cambridge, and Dover Castle ; of moulded pilasters at each side of the north doorway of Bradford-on-Avon ; and of the tower arch at St. Benet's, Cambridge ; of fluted window-jambs in the tower at Deerhurst ;

and of an ornamental string-course on the tower at Sompting.

Balusters.

Moulded stone balusters, turned in a lathe, and bulging out in the middle, are employed in Saxon architecture instead of the plain cylindrical columns seen in later styles. There are a large number at St. Alban's Abbey, others preserved in the porch at Jarrow, and they are to be seen in most of the double-light belfry windows of Saxon towers. The mouldings are in low relief, and resemble those which find favour with wood-turners.

Sculpture.

Sculpture seems to have been very sparingly employed in Saxon architecture, the following being most of the known examples :—

Britford, Wiltshire : Jambs of archway decorated with flat slabs of scroll foliage and interlaced work in low relief.

Bradford-on-Avon, Wilts : Two slabs with angels built into west wall of nave over chancel arch.

Monkwearmouth, co. Durham : Frieze of sculptured animals, much defaced over doorway in west wall of tower ; pair of entwined serpents, with birds' heads in low relief, on jambs of doorway in west wall of tower.

Barnack, Northamptonshire : Three slabs, with scrolls of foliage and birds, built into north, south, and west walls of second story of tower.

Earl's Barton, Northamptonshire : Crosses in relief

over double windows in lower story of tower, and shallow arcading on impost of west doorway.

Offchurch, Northamptonshire: Serpent on arch stone of window.

St. Botolph's, Sussex: Impost of chancel arch.

Sompting, Sussex: Rude scrolls of foliage on imposts of tower arch.

Stanton Lacy, Shropshire: Cross in relief over north door of nave.

Deerhurst, Gloucestershire: Figure of saint in niche over inner doorway of tower; beasts' heads forming terminations of hood-moulding of west door of nave; font covered with spiral patterns.

St. Benet's, Cambridge: Blocks of stone, with beasts in relief, forming terminations of hood-mouldings of tower arch.

Daglingworth, Gloucestershire: Three slabs built into west wall of chancel, one on each side of chancel arch, and the other above the crown, with representations of St. Peter holding key, Christ enthroned holding cross, and the Crucifixion.

Langford, Oxfordshire: Crucifix built into east wall of south porch.

Headbourne Worthy, Hampshire: Crucifix.

Hackness, Yorkshire: Impost of chancel arch, with lacertine beasts interlaced.

Ledsham, Yorkshire: Doorway in tower, with interlaced work on imposts, and scroll foliage round arch.

Crypts.

Crypts of Saxon date exist at Brixworth, Northamptonshire; Wing, Buckinghamshire; Repton,

Derbyshire; and Hexham, Northumberland. At Lastingham, in Yorkshire, there is a very early Norman crypt, probably built on the site of an earlier Saxon one. Similar crypts are to be seen beneath the high altars in the early churches in Italy and France, where they are used to contain the relics of saints and martyrs. In the Italian churches the high altar is not placed against the east wall of the chancel, as in England, but in the middle of the apse, and is covered over with a stone canopy called a valdachino. The crypt below is called a " confessio," [1] and an episcopal chair is placed against the middle of the wall of the apse. A chair of this kind of stone, with Hiberno-Saxon ornament upon it, is preserved at Hexham. The crypts at Ripon and at Hexham are very similar in ground-plan and general design. The principal chamber is rectangular, covered with a barrel vault, and surrounded by a passage on the north, south, and west sides, with doorways leading into the inner chamber on the south and west. There are several niches in the walls for placing lamps in. The size of the chamber at Ripon is 11 ft. 3 in. long by 7 ft. 9 in. wide, and that at Hexham 13 ft. 4 in. long by 8 ft. wide. The outer passage is connected with the church above by three staircases. The doorways are 6 ft. 3 in. high, with round heads cut out of the solid masonry. The

[1] "Sub altari majori . . . ubi Sanctorum martyrum corpora requiescunt, qui martyrium sive confessio appellatur."— Augustine, serm. 101, de Diversis, lib. xx, There is a very early "confessio" in the cathedral of St. James at Compostella in Spain, resembling those at Ripon and Hexham (see plan given in Rohault de Fleury's "La Messe," vol. ii. p. 83).

heads of the niches at Ripon are round, but those at Hexham flat.[1] Both of these crypts are supposed to have been built by St. Wilfrid, and the one at Ripon is known as St. Wilfrid's Needle. The crypt at Repton, Derbyshire, is about 17 ft. square, with a vaulted roof, supported on round-arched flat ribs springing from four twisted columns in the middle, and eight pilasters projecting from the side walls.[2] It is supposed to be a part of the conventual church destroyed by the Danes, who wintered here A.D. 874, at which time Eadburga, daughter of Eadulph, king of the East Angles, was abbess. The crypt at Lastingham is a square of about 22 ft., with a roof like that at Repton, supported on four low columns and round-arched flat ribs, but the details appear to be early Norman rather than Saxon.[3] This place derives its chief interest from having been founded by Cedd, brother of St. Chad, A.D. 648, and from the stone church recorded by Bede to have been built there.

Fonts.

It has been doubted whether there are any Saxon fonts still remaining, but specimens with early inscriptions are to be found at Potterne, Wiltshire, and Little Billing, Northamptonshire. Others with spirals, key-patterns, and interlaced work, similar to the ornament in the Hiberno-Saxon MSS. occur at

[1] For full description of these crypts, see paper by Mr. J. T. Micklethwaite in the "Journal of the British Archæological Institute," vol. xxxix. p. 346.

[2] See plan in S. Lyson's "Magna Britannia," vol. v. p. 219.

[3] "Associated Architectural Societies' Reports," vol. xii. p. 203.

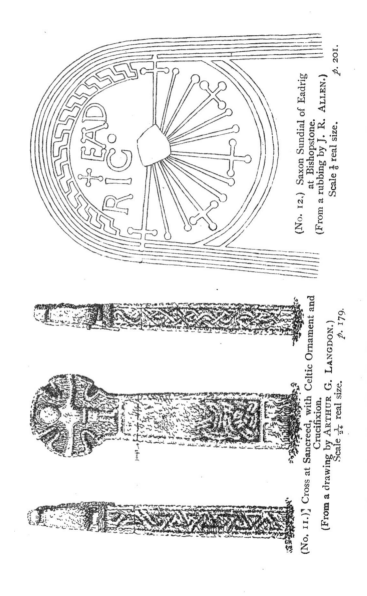

(No. 12.) Saxon Sundial of Eadrig at Bishopstone. (From a rubbing by J. R. ALLEN.) Scale ⅛ real size. *p.* 201.

(No. 11.) Cross at Sancreed, with Celtic Ornament and Crucifixion. (From a drawing by ARTHUR G. LANGDON.) Scale 1/24 real size. *p.* 179.

Deerhurst, Gloucestershire; Edgmond and Bucknell, Shropshire; Penmon, Anglesey; and South Hayling, Hampshire.

Sundials.

Before the invention of clocks a sundial was a very necessary adjunct to every religious establishment, for the purpose of marking the ecclesiastical divisions of the day and ensuring punctual attendance at the various religious services. Most Saxon churches appear to have been provided with a sundial, which was built into the wall above the south doorway of the nave. At Daglingworth, Gloucestershire, there is one in this position still *in situ*. It consists of a small stone, 1 ft. square, with a circle formed by two incised lines upon it. The lower half of the circle is divided into four segments by radial lines marked at the end with a cross. In the centre there is a hole for the gnomon, which has disappeared. The Saxons were evidently unacquainted with the correct way of setting out a sundial, as, from want of geometrical knowledge, all the hour angles are made equal instead of getting larger as they approach the horizontal diameter of the circle. Other simple sundials of this class occur at Winchester, Corhampton, and Warnford, Hampshire. Saxon sundials are often inscribed with the name of the maker. Thus we learn that Eadrig made the one at Bishopstone in Sussex; Lothan the one at Edston, near Pickering, in Yorkshire, which is also inscribed above, "Orologium viatorum" (the wayfarer's clock);[1] Hawarth the one

[1] Prof. G. F. Browne, of Cambridge, informs me that there is a drawing of a sundial, with these very words upon it, in the

at Kirkdale in Yorkshire, which has in addition over the top, the inscription :- –

"This is dœges solmera cet ilcum tide."
(This is the index of the sun's day and each of its hours.)

Dedication Stones.

In several Saxon churches the original dedication stone still exists. The most ancient one is at Jarrow, showing that the church was dedicated to St. Paul on the 9th of the kalends of May, in the 15th year of King Egfrith, and the 4th year of the Abbot Ceolfrid, under God the founder of the said church. Egfrith was King of Northumbria from A.D. 670 to 685, so that the date is fixed at A.D. 684. Ceolfrid was first abbot of St. Paul's, Jarrow, under Benedict Biscop. The dedication stone at Kirkdale, in Yorkshire, is on each side of the sundial, and bears an inscription in the old English tongue, to the effect that, "Orm, son of Gamal, bought St. Gregory's Church when it was all ruined and fallen down, and caused it to be made new from the ground to Christ and St. Gregory, in the days of Eadward the King and Tosti the Earl." Tosti was Earl of Northumbria A.D. 1055–1065, and Orm was murdered by his orders A.D. 1064, and therefore the date cannot be later than this year.

A dedication stone was dug up near Deerhurst Church in the last century, and is now preserved amongst the Arundel Marbles at Oxford. It has a curious Irish "Liber S. Isidori," in the library at Bâle, in Switzerland. There is also a drawing of a Saxon sundial in the Eleventh Century Psalter (Tib. c. vi.), fol. 7, in the British Museum.

Latin inscription upon it, of which the following is a translation :—

"Earl Odda ordered this royal building to be constructed and dedicated in honour of the Holy Trinity for the soul of his cousin Ælfric, who died at this place. It was Eadred the Bishop who dedicated it on the 3rd of April, in the fourteenth year of St. Eadward, king of England (*i.e.*, A.D. 1053)."

We learn from the Saxon Chronicle that Odda was Earl of Devon, Somerset, Dorset, and the Welsh (A.D. 1051–1056). Ælfric, Odda's brother, died at Deerhurst in 1053.

Other Saxon dedication stones of less historical interest exist at St. Mary's, Castlegate, York ; Aldborough, Yorkshire ; and in the recently-discovered chapel at Deerhurst.

Interior Decorations.

The interior decorations of the Saxon churches now existing have entirely disappeared, but we learn from the writings of Bede that they were adorned with pictures of Scripture subjects, and that the windows were glazed. In his "Lives of the Holy Abbots," he tells us that Benedict Biscop brought back from Rome, on one occasion (A.D. 678), for his monastery at Monkwearmouth pictures of the Virgin, the twelve Apostles, scenes from the Gospels and from the Apocalypse ; and on another (A.D. 685), pictures of Our Lord's history, to be hung round the Lady Chapel at Monkwearmouth, and Old and New Testament types for the church at Jarrow. Richard of Hexham also describes the walls and the capitals of Wilfrid's Church at Hexham (founded A.D. 674), as being decorated with histories and pictures, and various figures sculptured in relief. At the second Council of Calcuth, in Northumberland, held in A.D. 816, a canon was issued requiring every bishop, before consecrating a church, to see painted on the walls, or over the altar thereof, a portrait of the patron saint.

Sepulchral and other Monuments.

The Pagan Anglo-Saxons buried their dead either in large cemeteries, which was the more common practice, or under mounds of earth in isolated positions. The termination "low," occurring in the names of many places in England, especially in Derbyshire, indicates that a Saxon tumulus existed there at some time or other, the "low" being the modern form of the Saxon "hlœw," meaning a hillock. A good instance occurs in the name Taplow, on the Thames, where a Saxon burial mound was opened a few years ago, and found to contain some valuable antiquities, now deposited in the British Museum. The Saxon cemeteries were generally situated on high ground, and the graves were very much like those in a churchyard of the present day, containing the body of the deceased lying at full length on its back in full dress. If the body was that of a man it was surrounded by his sword, shield, drinking-cup, and often a wooden bucket hooped with bronze ; if it was that of a woman she was buried with her personal ornaments, the bunch of keys at her girdle or any other object she may have valued during her lifetime. In Kent and the south of England the body was deposited in the grave entire, but in East Anglia cremation appears to have prevailed. One of the best collections of antiquities derived from Saxon cemeteries is that formed by Dr. Faussett, now in the Mayer Museum, at Liverpool. Descriptions of researches amongst Saxon cemeteries will be found in Douglas's "Nenia"; W. M. Wylie's "Fairford Graves"; B. Faussett's "Inventorium Sepulchrale"; Ackerman's "Remains of Pagan Saxondom"; Roach Smith's "Collectanea Antiqua"; and the proceedings of the various archæological societies. The Pagan Saxons marked the position of their graves by erecting a mound of earth above the place where each body was interred, and stone monuments, either erect or recumbent, seem to have been quite unknown.[1] With the introduction of Christianity the custom of depositing grave-goods with the body and cremation was given up, and the age of inscribed and ornamented stone sepulchral monuments begins. It has been pointed out in a previous chapter that rude pillar stones with inscriptions in Oghams or debased Latin capitals do not occur in the Anglo-Saxon parts of Great Britain. All the monuments we have now to deal with are carefully wrought into the shape of an erect cross, a flat cross slab, or a recumbent hog-backed stone, sculptured with various kinds of Hiberno-Saxon ornament, and often inscribed in Runes, well-formed Latin capitals, or Saxon minuscules. Our knowledge concerning these monuments is derived by a minute

[1] In Prof. Stephen's "Old Northern Runic Monuments," the only stones with Runic inscriptions attributed to the Pagan period are two at Sandwich in Kent.

examination of the following points : (1) the forms of the letters of the inscriptions, the linguistic and grammatical peculiarities of the language in which they are written, the formulæ, and the names mentioned ; (2) the style of the ornament; and (3) the symbolism of the figure sculpture. As the inscribed stones afford a basis for classifying the rest according to their age, we will begin with them first.

The Runic alphabet, or futhorc as it is called, from the first seven letters, is of Scandinavian origin. It is still a matter of doubt at what period Runes were invented, and whether they were derived from Latin or Greek letters. Those who are interested in the matter may consult Canon Isaac Taylor's "Greeks and Goths," from which the following particulars are chiefly taken. The Runic futhorc is divided, like the Ogham alphabet, into groups three in number called respectively Frey's aett, Hagel's aett, and Tyr's aett, from the letters F, H, and T, with which each group begins. There are several different varieties of Runes, all founded on the old Gothic futhorc, as follows :—

Gothic Runes.—Used in the earliest inscriptions in all countries, of which 200 are known dating from the third to the sixth century. Futhorc consists of twenty-four letters. Occurs as a futhorc upon a bracteate of the fourth century found at Vadstena, Sweden, and on a brooch from Charnay, Burgundy.

Anglian Runes.—Used on Northumbrian monuments from the seventh to the tenth century. Futhorc contains four to twelve additional letters. Occurs as a futhorc on a sixth-century sword found in the Thames, and in MSS. of the eighth and ninth centuries.

RUNIC FUTHORCS.

Name.	Value.	Gothic.	Anglian.	Scand.	Manx.	
Feh	F					Frey's Aett.
Ur	U					
Thorn	Th					
Os	O					
Rad	R					
Cen	C					
Gebo	G					
Wen	W					
Hagel	H					Hagel's Aett.
Nod	N					
Is	I					
Yr, Ar	Yor A					
Eoh	Eo					
Perd	P					
Ilix	A					
Sigil	S					
Tir	T					Tyrs Aett.
Berc	B					
Ech	E					
Man	M					
Lago	L					
Ing	Ng					
Dag	D					
Othil	O					
(No. 13.)		A	Æ	Ü	Ea	

Scandinavian Runes.—Used in 2,000 inscriptions, found chiefly in Norway, Sweden, and Denmark from the tenth to the sixteenth century. Futhorc contains sixteen letters. Occurs as a futhorc on a slab at Maeshowe, Orkney, and on a twelfth-century font at Bœrse, Denmark.

Manx Runes.—Used in twenty inscriptions in the Isle of Man and the islands off the coast of Scotland. Futhorc contains fourteen letters.

Tree Runes.—Used in cryptic inscriptions at Rök and Rotbrunna, Sweden; Maeshowe, Orkney; and Hackness, Yorkshire. In Tree Runes, the futhorc being divided into three groups thus, Frey's aett FUTHORC, Hagl's aett HNIAS, and Tyr's aett TBLMY, an upright stem or tree trunk was taken, and the number of branches to the left denoted the aett or family, and the number of branches to the right the position in that family.

Bind Runes.—Used in an inscription at Kirk Andreas, Isle of Man. These Runes consist of several letters on one stem line.

The following is a list of the Christian monuments with inscriptions in Anglian Runes in England[1] and Scotland:—

Erect Crosses:—

Bewcastle	Cumberland
Chester-le-Street	Durham
Crowle	Lincolnshire
Lancaster	Lancashire
Alnmouth	Northumberland
Collingham	Yorkshire

---

[1] A newly-discovered Runic inscription from Overchurch, near Upton, in Cheshire, has been recently described by Prof. G. F. Browne.

Erect Crosses (continued) :—

Hackness	Yorkshire
Thornhill	,,
Ruthwell	Dumfriesshire

Sepulchral Slabs :—

Hartlepool	Durham
Dover	Kent

Recumbent Hog-backed Stone :—

Falstone	Northumberland

Fragments :—

Monkwearmouth	Durham
Leeds	Yorkshire

The crosses at Bewcastle and at Ruthwell are far the finest Rune inscribed monuments in Great Britain, and the design of both is so similar that if they are not the work of the same artist they are certainly of the same school and period. Unfortunately the inscription on the former is so much obliterated that it cannot be read with any degree of certainty, and the inscription on the latter contains no names or facts which help to throw light upon its age. All that now remains of the Bewcastle cross is the shaft, 14 ft. 6 in. high. The north and south sides are ornamented with panels of interlaced work, chequer patterns, and scrolls of foliage, there being five lines of Anglian Runes on the horizontal bands between the panels. The east side has a continuous scroll of foliage with animals running from top to bottom, and no inscriptions. The west side has sculptures of St. John carrying the Agnus Dei, Christ, and a man holding a hawk. There are single lines of Runes on two of the horizontal bands between the upper panels and nine lines on the space between the lower ones. The inscriptions have been conjecturally made out by the Rev. J. Maughan, and translations given by the late Dr. D. H. Haigh, in the "Archæologia Æliana," vol. i., new series, and by Prof. G. Stephens in his "Old Northern Runic Monuments." If these authorities are to be believed the inscriptions record the erection of the cross to Alcfrith, King of Northumbria (*circa* A.D. 653) and mention the names of several of his relations.

The romantic history of the Ruthwell cross has been graphically related by Dr. J. Anderson in his "Scotland in Early Christian Times" (second series). He tells us how it was probably first set up at the time when the ancient kingdom of Northumbria was at the zenith of its power, of the indignities it suffered at the hands of bigoted Protestants, who broke it up as a Popish relic in the seventeenth century, of its re-erection in the churchyard by the Rev. Dr. Duncan, in 1823, and of the interesting particulars connected with the decipherment of the Runic inscriptions by Mr. J. M. Kemble, the great Saxon scholar. The last scene in the drama took place in the Jubilee year of the reign of Queen Victoria (1887) when it was placed under cover within the church in a chamber specially built for the purpose under the auspices of the present Minister, the Rev. J. McFarlan, who has written an admirable little brochure on the "The Ruthwell Cross." On the front and back are scenes from the New Testament, and from the Apocryphal Gospels with explanatory Latin inscriptions in Roman capital letters. On the two sides are scrolls of foliage and birds with

P

inscriptions in Anglian Runes across the top and down the sides. The meaning of the inscriptions was first correctly made out by Mr. J. M. Kemble, in 1840, and he subsequently was able to show that it formed portion of an Anglo-Saxon poem, entitled "The Dream of the Holy Rood," a MS. copy of which was discovered in 1823 by Professor Blume, at Vercelli, in the north of Italy. The authorship of this poem has been attributed by Professor G. Stephens, of Copenhagen, to Caedmon, on the strength of some Runes on the head of the Ruthwell cross, which have been read by him and the late Dr. Daniel Haigh to mean,—

" Caedmon me made."

All trace of the name has, however, disappeared, and it is exceedingly doubtful if it ever existed, especially as the poem in the Vercelli codex is believed to have been written by Cynewulf, whose name occurs in Runes distributed here and there amongst the other letters in the book.[1] The fact of Caedmon's having possibly not been the author of " The Dream of the Holy Rood " can in no way affect the merit of the composition, nor can it detract from the value of a monument bearing the longest inscription known in the Old English tongue and whose sculptured decorations bear witness to the high culture existing at that early period amongst the Northumbrian Christians. The more important crosses, such as those at Ruthwell and Bewcastle,

[1] See J. M. Kemble, "On Anglo-Saxon Runes," in the " Archæologia," vol. xxviii. p. 361.

(No. 14.) Cross of Gilsuith and Berhtsuith at Thornhill, with Inscription in Anglian Runes.

(From a rubbing by J. R. ALLEN.)   Scale ¼ real size.   *p.* 211.

were evidently not sepulchral, but probably erected to commemorate some illustrious personage, and to encourage a devotional frame of mind by setting before the congregation scenes from the Gospels. The cross, formerly at Lancaster, and now in the British Museum, seems to have been of another type. It has no figure sculpture, only interlaced ornament, and is inscribed

> " Gibidœth foræ Cünibalth Cuthbærehting."
> (Pray for Cunibalth, Cuthbert's son.)

The inscription on the cross shaft found at Alnmouth, and now in the Duke of Northumberland's Museum at Alnwick, gives us the name of the maker and scribe, a most unusual circumstance. It runs thus :—

> " Myredah meh wo,
>   Hludweg meh feg."
> (Myredah me wrought,
> Hludwyd me inscribed.)

The inscription on the bottom of one of the cross shafts at Thornhill is very distinct, being as follows :—

" + Gilsuith arærde æft Bersuithe becun at bergi ; Gibidad der saule."

(+ Gilsuith erected this monument over his burial mound to Bersuithe.   Pray for his soul.)

The sepulchral slabs generally have a cross simply, or a cross with the addition of the Alpha and Omega, and the name of the deceased alone in Anglian Runes. Thus at Hartlepool we have the slabs of Hildithryth and of Hildigyth, and at Dover that of Gyoslheard. In the museum of the Society of Antiquaries at Newcastle-on-Tyne there is a diminutive hog-backed recumbent stone with a biliteral inscription in minuscules and Anglian Runes, which reads as follows :—

"— Eomer thæ sættæ æfter Roethberhtæ becun æfter Eomer. Gebidad der saule."
(+ Eomer erected this to Rœthberht, a beacon to Eomer. Pray for his soul.)

A small wedge-shaped stone, found at Monkwearmouth, is now preserved in the British Museum. On one side it has a man carved, and on the other two men holding up a rectangular object (perhaps a book) over a cross placed between them. Above is a small panel with the name Tidfirth inscribed in Anglian Runes.

The crosses in the Isle of Man are all sepulchral, and twenty of them are inscribed. One example from the cross of Arinbjörg at Kirk Andreas will be sufficient to give an idea of the rest :—

"Sont Ulf hin Suarti raisti krus thona aftir Arinbiaurk kuino sina."
(Sandulf the Black erected this cross to his wife Arinbjörg.)

Complete readings of all the inscriptions will be found in P. M. C. Kermode's "Catalogue of the Manx Crosses" and in the Rev. J. G. Cumming's "Runic and other Remains of the Isle of Man."

The Latin capitals used in Saxon times differ from those on the Celtic pillar stones in being more regularly formed, and have certain peculiarities not found in Roman inscriptions, such as the square C the diamond-shaped O, the S made like a Z reversed and new varieties of the letters D, H, M, N, &c. In

UTR RISTI KRUS THONO AFT FROKA.

(No. 15.) Cross of Utr and Froka, at Kirk Braddan, with
Inscription in Manx Runes.
(From a rubbing by J. R. ALLEN.) Scale $\frac{1}{6}$ real size. *p.* 212

the later inscriptions special symbols are invented for &, W, Dh., &c.

There are inscriptions in Latin capitals on Christian Saxon monuments at the following places :—

Crosses :—

    Carlisle Cathedral, Cumberland.
    Bishop Auckland, Durham.
    Monkwearmouth,   ,,
    Alnmouth, Northumberland.
    Dewsbury, Yorkshire.
    Hackness,   ,,
    Ripon,   ,,
    Thornhill,   ,,
    Wycliffe,   ,,
    York,   ,,
    Trevillet, Cornwall.
    Ruthwell, Dumfriesshire.

Sepulchral Slabs :—

    Hartlepool, Durham.
    Wensley, Yorkshire.

Headstone :—

    Whitchurch, Hampshire.

Most of these inscriptions are in Latin, although there are a few in the vernacular, as at Wycliffe and at Trevillet. A great part are also in so fragmentary a condition that little can be made out beyond the names. In the York Museum we have a small cross shaft brought from Ripon set up to

" + ADHVSE PRB "

(+ Adhuse, Bishop);

and another bearing the words,—

". . . DIT AD MEMORIAM SCORVM."

(. . . to the memory of the Saints.)

A fragment of a cross from Jarrow, now in the Newcastle Museum, is inscribed,—

".... BERCHTI ... EDVERI ... CRVCEM,"

from which it has been conjectured that it was intended to commemorate Huetbert, Abbot of Jarrow.

Another fragment in the porch at Jarrow has the inscription,—

"... IN HOC SINGVLA(RI) (AN)NO VITA REDDITVR MVNDO."

The cross shaft which formerly existed between Greta Bridge and Wycliffe has been lost, but from an engraving of it given in Gough's edition of "Camden's Britannia" it recorded the fact of the erection of a monument to Berchtuini by Bœda. The language is the early Northumbrian dialect, and the formula of the same class as those at Thornhill, already given. From an historical point of view, perhaps, the three fragmentary inscribed cross shafts at Hackness are the most interesting of all, since the names mentioned are those of persons belonging to the monastery founded by St. Hilda at Hacanos, in the year of her death A.D. 680, as recorded by Bede ("Eccl. Hist.," bk. iv. ch. xxiii). Fragment No. 1 has knotwork on one side and scrolls on the other ; on the front an inscription conjecturally containing the name of Huethberg, who is called Mater Amantissima (most blessed mother) ; and on the back an inscription mentioning the name of Oedilburg, who is styled "beata" (blessed). Dr. D. H. Haigh identifies " Œthilburg with the Abbess Æthelburg, who accompanied Ælfflæd to Driffield on her visit to her dying brother Aldfrith, in 705, and whose name follows Ælfflæd's in the 'Liber Vitæ.'"[1] He believes that Huethbeg is the Wetburg referred to in the correspondence of St. Boniface, letters Nos. xxxii. and xxxiii., written A.D. 717 to 723. Fragment No. 2 has dragons on one side and cryptic letters of unknown meaning on the back, and on the front an inscription in capitals, mentioning the names of Trecea, Bosa, and Abatissa Œdilburga. Fragment No. 3 has the bust of a female on the front, with an inscription above read by Dr. Haigh as "BVGGA"; and on the back an inscription partly in Anglian and partly in Tree Runes.

As examples of sepulchral slabs with inscriptions in Latin capitals we may take those at Hartlepool, discovered in the years 1833 and 1843, on the site of the ancient cemetery of the monastery founded by St. Heiu at Heruteu, over which Hild presided as abbess until she migrated to Whitby, A.D. 658 (Bede, " Eccl. Hist.," bk. iii. ch. 24; and iv. 23). The cemetery was accidentally found when digging the foundations of some houses in a field called Cross Close about 135 yards south-east of the ancient Chapel of St. Hild. Several skeletons of males and females of large stature were uncovered at a depth of about 3 ft. 6 in. below the surface, lying in rows upon the surface of the limestone rock. With them were found nine sepulchral slabs of much smaller size than usual, varying from 5 in. to 12 in. square. All are

[1] "The Monasteries of S. Heiu and S. Hild," in the "Journal of the Yorkshire Archæological and Topographical Association," vol. ii. p. 374.

marked with crosses, and two have the Alpha and Omega in addition. Two bear inscriptions in Anglian Runes; two in minuscules; and five in capitals. The inscriptions on the latter are as follows :—

No. 1. ". . . HOC LOCO . . . REQVIESCIT."
(. . . rests in this place.)
No. 2. " KANEGNEUB."
(Kanegneub.)
No. 3. " EDILUINI."
(Ediluini.)
No. 4. "ŌRA PRO VERMUND & TORHTSUID."
(Pray for Vermund and Torhtsuid.)
No. 5. "ORATE PRO EDILUINI.
ORATE PRO VERMUND ET TORHTSUID."
(Pray for Ediluini.
Pray for Vermund and Torhtsuid.)

There are two interesting sepulchral cross slabs at Wensley, in Yorkshire, inscribed in capitals, one bearing the name " DONFRID," and the other " EATBEREHT ET ARUINI."

There is only one instance known of a Saxon headstone inscribed in capitals, which is at Whitchurch, Hampshire. The stone is 1 ft. 10 in. high by 1 ft. wide by 9 in. thick. On the front is carved a bust of Christ, with the cruciferous nimbus, holding a book in one hand and giving the benediction with the other; and on the back is an elegant scroll ornament. The top of the stone is semi-circular, with the following inscription in capitals round the edge :—

" + HIC CORPVS FRIOBERGAE REQVIESCIT IN PACEM SEPVLTVM."
(Here lies the body of Frithburga, buried in peace.)

(No. 16.)
Sepulchral Slab of Vermund and Torhtsuid from Hartlepool,
now in the Newcastle Museum, with Inscription in
Saxon Capitals.
(From a paper cast by R BLAIR.)
Scale ½ real size.

We have shown in a previous chapter that nearly all the inscriptions found on stones in the Celtic portions of Great Britain from the 7th to the 11th century are in minuscules.   In the Saxon and Danish districts, on the contrary, the inscriptions are generally either in Latin capitals or Runes, and even when minuscules occur they are often mixed with capitals. The following is a list of the Christian monuments in England with minuscule inscriptions :—

Crosses :—
> Beckermet St. Bridget, Cumberland.
> Dewsbury, Yorkshire.
> Hawkswell,   ,,
> Yarm,   ,,
> St. Neot, Cornwall.
> Lanherne   ,,

Sepulchral Slabs :—
> Hartlepool, Durham.
> Billingham,   ,,
> Camborne, Cornwall.
> Pendarves,   ,,

Hog-backed recumbent Monuments :—
> Falstone, Northumberland.

The inscription on the cross at Beckermet St. Bridget's is so obliterated that it would be hopeless to attempt to read it ; but notwithstanding this, the late Dr. D. H. Haigh endeavoured to show that it commemorated Tuda the Bishop of Lindisfarne who is recorded by Bede (" Eccl. Hist.," bk. iii., ch. xxvii.) to have died of the plague, A.D. 664, at a monastery called Pœgnalœch.   A portion of the head of a cross found at Dewsbury is now preserved in the British

Museum, bearing the following inscription in minuscules :—

> ". . . rhtæ becun æfter Beornæ ; Gibiddad der saule."
> (. . . rhtæ erected this monument to the Prince. Pray for his soul.)

The inscription on the cross shaft found in use as a mangle-weight at Yarm, and now removed to the Cathedral Library at Durham, is of a similar kind. It runs thus :—

> ". . . r . . mberecht + sac + alla + signum æfter his breodera ysetæ."
> (. . . r . . mberecht + Bishop + This sign after his brother set.)

The cross at Hawkswell has a small panel on the shaft with the inscription :

> " Hæc est crux Sc Gacobi."
> (This is the cross of Sanctus Gacobus.)

The minuscule inscriptions on the cross slabs do not differ from those in capitals and Runes already mentioned. The bi-literal stone at Falstone has been referred to when dealing with its Runic inscription.

In the foregoing description of the inscribed Christian monuments in the Anglo-Saxon portions of Great Britain it has been found convenient to divide them into three classes according to whether the letters are Runes, capitals, or, minuscules, and a sufficient number of typical examples of each kind having been given, we will now review the whole, in order to show what information may be gained from the formulæ and names which occur. On the

sepulchral slabs the only name given is that of the
deceased, and the person who made it, or by whose
orders it was made, is omitted altogether. The case
of the erect crosses is, however, different. In the
Isle of Man, for instance, the setter-up of the monument is always mentioned, the formula employed
being,—

" A raisti crus thana aftir B."
(A raised this cross to the memory of B) ;

or,—

" A raist runar thenar aftir B."
(A raised these runes to the memory of B.)

In the Northumbrian inscriptions we have a similar
formula, except that the monument is called a
" becun," thus :—

" A thæ settæ æfter B becun æfter."
(A set up this to B a monument to his memory.)

In the Latin inscriptions the word "crux" only
occurs twice, at Jarrow and at Hawkswell. The
maker of the cross is given in one instance, at
Alnmouth. On a sculptured gravestone, with an
inscription in Scandinavian Runes, found in St.
Paul's Churchyard, and now in the Guildhall
Museum, the formula is,—

" A let lekia stin thensi."
(A caused this stone to be laid.)

But there is nothing to show that the monument is
a Christian one. A request to pray for the soul of
the dead is not uncommon on both the stones with
Latin and with vernacular inscriptions. Thus "Orate

pro A " (Pray for A) is to be seen on the cross-shaft at Hackness, and on sepulchral slabs at Billingham and at Hartlepool; and " Gibidœth foræ A " (Pray for A), at Lancaster. The word "soul" is added in the inscriptions at Falstone, at Thornhill, and at Dewsbury, where the formula is "Gibidad der saule " (Pray for his soul). On the base of the cross at St. Neot we have,—

> " A rogavit pro anima B."
> (A has prayed for the soul of B.)

And on a sepulchral slab at Camborne,—

> " A jussit hec altare pro anima sua."
> (A ordered this slab to be prepared for his soul.)

Very similar to this is the formula,—

> " A raisti crus thano fur salu sini "
> (A raised this cross for his soul),

at Kirk Michael, in the Isle of Man. "Requiescit" occurs in two cases at Monkwearmouth, where the words are,—

> " Hic in sepulcro requiescit corpore A."
> (Here lies in the tomb the body of A.)

And at Whitchurch,—

> " Hic corpus A requiescit in pacem sepultum."
> (Here lies the body of A, buried in peace.)

The relationship between the deceased and the erector of the monument is hardly ever mentioned on the English stones, there being only one instance, at Yarm, but in the Isle of Man the practice is very common. The title, profession, or station of the deceased occurs occasionally; at Monkwearmouth and at Ripon we have PRB (Bishop); at Yarm, "Sac" (Bishop); at Hawkswell SCS (Saint); at Collingham "Cyning" (King); and at Kirk Michael, in the Isle of Man, "Smith" (Smith). On some of the Manx crosses descriptive adjectives are added after the names, such as the Black, the Red, and so on.

A list of something like fifty-seven names are to be obtained from the inscribed monuments of the Anglo-Saxon Christian period, which are enumerated below :—

Name.	Place.	County.	Class of Monument.	Class of Letter.
Adhuse........	Ripon	Yorksh	Cross shaft	C
Aelgeld	Lanteglos	Cornwall ..	,, ,,	C
Aelnat	Trevillet	Cornwall ..	,, ,,	C
Aelwyneys	Lanteglos	Cornwall ..	,, ,,	C
Aruini	Wensley	Yorksh	Sep. slab	C
Baeda	Wycliffe	Yorksh	Cross shaft	C
*Berchtgyd	Hartlepool	Durham ..	Sep. slab	M
Berhtsuith	Thornhill......	Yorksh	Cross shaft	R
Berchtuini	Wycliffe	Yorksh	,, ,,	C
Bosa	Hackness	Yorksh	,, ,,	C
*Bregusuid (2)..	Hartlepool	Durham ..	Sep. slab	M
*Bugga	Hackness......	Yorksh	Cross shaft	C
Cuthbercht	Lancaster	Lancash ..	,, ,,	R
Cynibalth	Lancaster	Lancash ..	,, ,,	R
Donfrid	Wensley	Yorksh	Sep. slab	C
Doniert	St. Neot	Cornwall ..	Cross base	M
Eadmund	Chester-le-Street	Durham ..	Cross shaft	C
Eadred........	Thornhill......	Yorksh	,, ,,	R
Eadulf........	Alnmouth	Northumb .	,, ,,	C
Eatbercht	Wensley	Yorksh	Sep. slab	C
Eata..........	Thornhill......	Yorksh	Cross shaft	k
Ediluini	Hartlepool	Durham ..	Sep. slab	C
Ethelb	Thornhill......	Yorksh	Cross shaft	R
Eomer	Falstone	Northumb .	Hog-back'd stone	M
*Frithburga	Whitchurch ..	Hampsh ..	Head-stone ..	C
Gacobus	Hawkswell	Yorksh	Cross shaft	M
Genered	Lanteglos	Cornwall ..	,, ,,	C
Gilsuith	Thornhill......	Yorksh	,, ,,	R
Gnira	Dearham	Cumberland	Recumbent stone	R

Name.	Place.	County.	Class of Monument.	Class of Letter.
Gyoslheard ..	Dover	Kent	Sep. slab	R
*Heiu	Healaugh ....:	Yorksh	,, ,, ...	C
Hereberecht ..	Monkwearmouth	Durham ..	,, ,, ...	C
Hilddigyth	Hartlepool	Durham ..	,, ,, ...	R
Hildithryth....	Hartlepool	Durham ..	,, ,, ...	R
Hludwyg	Alnmouth	Northumb.	Cross shaft	R
Hroethberht ..	Falstone	Northumb.	Hog-back'd stone	M R
*Huaethburga ..	Hackness	Yorksh	Cross shaft	C
Kanegneub ..	Hartlepool	Durham ..	Sep. slab	C
Konal	St. Paul's	London....	Head-stone ..	R
Leviut	Camborne	Cornwall ..	Sep. slab	C
Madug	Healaugh	Yorksh	,, ,, ...	C
Myredeh	Alnmouth	Northumb.	Cross shaft	R
*Oedilburga	Hackness	Yorksh	,, ,, ...	C
Onlaf	Leeds	,, ...	Fragment	R
Oswini	Collingham ..	,, ...	Cross shaft	R
Osber	Thornhill......	,, ...	Fragment	C
Runhol........	Lanherne......	Cornwall ..	Cross shaft	C
Tidfirth	Monkwearmouth	Durham ..	Small stone....	R
Tolfihn	Carlisle	Cumberland		R
Torhtsuid	Hartlepool	Durham ..	Sep. slab	C
Trecea	Hackness	Yorksh	Cross shaft	C
Tuki..........	St. Paul's	London....	Head-stone ..	R
Vermund	Hartlepool	Durham ..	Sep. slab	C
.... berchti..	Jarrow	,, ..	Cross head	C
.... edueri ..	Jarrow	,, ..	,, ,, ...	C
..˙.. mberecht	Yarm	Yorksh	Cross shaft	M
.... rht	Dewsbury	Yorksh	Cross head	M

NOTE.—(C) stands for capitals, (M) for minuscules, and (R) for Runes. The names marked with an asterisk are those of females.

Most of the names in this list are such as we know to have been in common use amongst the Anglo-Saxons. The terminations which occur most frequently are ...bercht, as in Cuthbercht, Eatbercht, Hereberecht, and Hroethberht; ...burga, as in Frithburga, Huaethburga, and Oedilburga; ...yth, or ...uith, as in Bregusuid, Berhtsuith, Gilsuith, Hilddigyth, Hildithryth, and Torsuid; ...und, as in Eadmund and Vermund; and ...uini, as in Berchtuini and Etheluini. Some of the names have survived to the present day, such as Cuthbert and Edmund. Attempts have been made by Dr. D. H. Haigh and Prof. Geo. Stephens to identify many of the names with those of persons known in history, but the uncertainties attending an investigation of the kind are very great, arising from several causes. In the first place, the historical records of this early period are exceedingly scanty, and even when a name has been found in the records to correspond with one mentioned on an inscribed stone, it is difficult to show that the same individual is referred to in both cases, because in most of the inscriptions a single Christian name only is given, without any additional information by means of which a name of common occurrence can be distinguished from that belonging to some other person. In order to render the process of identification satisfactory, some connexion should be established between the individual mentioned in history and the locality where the inscription occurs. Dr. Haigh and Prof. Stephens generally either fail to do this, or there is some doubt as to the reading of the names in the inscription which renders the identification valueless.

On the Rune-inscribed crosses of the Isle of Man, the following thirty-three names are to be found :—

*Arinbjörg	Andreas.
*Asrith	German.
Athakans	Michael II.
Athisl	Michael III.
Björn	Andreas I.
Druian	Bride.
Dugald	Bride & Michael III.
Eaf	Baddan IV.
Feaac	Braddan I. & IV.

*Frithu	Michael V.
Froka	Braddan III.
Gaut	Andreas I. & Michael II.
Grim	Michael IV. & VI.
Inosruir	German.
Joalf	Michael V.
Kathmoil	Bride.
Liutulf	Ballaugh.
Malbrigd	Michael II.
*Malmuru	Michael III.
Malumkun	,,
Onon	Jurby.
Oulaibr	Ballaugh.
Rosketil	Braddan II.
Rumun	Michael IV.
Sandulf the Black	Andreas II.
Thurbjörn	Braddon V.
Thurith	Couchan.
Thurolf the Red	Michael V.
Thurlaf Neaki	Braddan IV.
Thurualtr	Andreas III.
Ufaac	Braddan I.
Ulf	Ballaugh.
Utr	Braddan III.

NOTE.—The names marked with an asterisk are those of females. The Roman numerals refer to the numbers in P. C. M. Kermode's "Catalogue of the Manx Crosses."

Nothing is known of any of the persons mentioned in these inscriptions, but the greater proportion of the names are Scandinavian, and belong to the time of the Norse invasions (A.D. 888 to 1266). A few, such as Dugald and Malbrigd (*i.e.*, the servant of St. Bridget), are Celtic.

Lastly, we come to the uninscribed Christian monuments of the Anglo-Saxon period, the chief interest of which lies in the forms of the crosses, the ornamental features, and the figure sculpture. There are in England about 230 localities where stones with

Hiberno-Saxon decoration are known to exist, and as more than one stone is found at many of the places, the total number of specimens of monuments, or fragments of monuments of this class, cannot fall far short of 400. It is impossible to give the exact number until a proper archæological survey has been made of the whole, either by Government or by the combined efforts of the various archæological societies throughout the country.

The following table shows approximately the geographical distribution of the localities where the stones occur over the forty counties of England :—

		Brought forward ...	100
Bedfordshire	1	Lincolnshire	11
Berkshire ....,	...	Middlesex	1
Buckinghamshire	...	Monmouthshire	1
Cambridgeshire	1	Norfolk	1
Cheshire	8	Northamptonshire ...	11
Cornwall	18	Northumberland	15
Cumberland	20	Nottinghamshire ...	1
Derbyshire	16	Oxfordshire	...
Devonshire	2	Rutland	2
Dorsetshire	...	Shropshire	...
Durham	19	Somersetshire	5
Essex	...	Staffordshire	9
Gloucestershire	1	Suffolk	...
Hampshire	1	Surrey	...
Herefordshire	...	Sussex	2
Hertfordshire	...	Warwickshire	...
Huntingdonshire	1	Westmoreland	1
Kent	2	Wiltshire	2
Lancashire	6	Worcestershire	1
Leicestershire	4	Yorkshire........	66
	100		229

It appears from the above that the stones are most numerous in those counties occupying the parts of England which in the ninth century constituted the southern halves of Northumbria and Strathclyde and the northern half of Mercia.

The Christian monuments of the Anglo-Saxon period consist of erect crosses with rectangular shafts, erect crosses with cylindrical shafts, erect headstones, recumbent hog-backed stones, and sepulchral slabs or coffin-lids.

A few of the crosses still occupy their original positions, others have been re-erected in modern times, and a large number are preserved inside churches in the fragmentary condition in which they have been found during restorations or alterations. Some of the smaller crosses may have been used to mark the head of a grave, but the larger ones are certainly not sepulchral. Like the high crosses of Ireland, they are decorated with Scriptural subjects, and were placed in churchyards or by the wayside, to encourage a devotional spirit in the mind of the passer-by, by calling his attention to the mysteries of the Christian religion. Belonging to this class are such crosses as that at Sandbach, in Cheshire, which has carved upon it the Crucifixion and other scenes from the life of Christ; that at Ilkley, in Yorkshire, with the symbols of the four Evangelists; that at Bewcastle, with the figures of Christ and St. John the Baptist; that at Bakewell, in Derbyshire, with the Crucifixion; and many others. Very few crosses are at present in perfect preservation, as in nearly all cases the head is wanting, having been either wantonly destroyed or, when composed of a separate stone from the shaft, the mortise and tenon having become loosened, the head has fallen off and been lost.

The crosses at Gosforth, at Deerham, and at Irton, in Cumberland, are amongst the few complete specimens which have survived. The ornamented bases or socket stones that are so universal in Ireland are exceedingly rare in England, although there is a fine one to be seen on Hartshead Moor, near Dewsbury, in Yorkshire. The chief peculiarity in the shape of the head of the typical Saxon cross is the absence of the surrounding ring. The ends of the arms are usually expanded, as in the Maltese cross. The shafts of the Saxon crosses are much more slender than those of the Irish crosses. The heights of these monuments vary from 4 ft. to 15 ft., the tallest being those at :—

	ft.	in.
Sandbach, Cheshire	22	0
Bewcastle, Cumberland	14	6
Gosforth, Cumberland	14	0
Leeds, Yorkshire	8	3
Ilkley, Yorkshire	8	4
Coppleston, Devon	10	6
Bakewell, Derbyshire	8	0
Eyam, Derbyshire	8	3

All the crosses in Ireland, Scotland, and Wales (with two exceptions) have rectangular shafts, but in the counties of Staffordshire, Cheshire, Derbyshire, Nottinghamshire, and Cumberland we find a peculiar type of cross with a cylindrical stem, unknown anywhere else. The following is a list of the places where they occur :—

Staffordshire—
Chebsey.
Checkley.
Ilam.
Leek.
Stoke-upon-Trent.

Staffordshire—
Wolverhampton.
Cheshire—
Chulow.
Lyme Park.
Macclesfield.

Q 2

Derbyshire—	*Cumberland—*
Bakewell.	Beckermet St. Bridget's.
Wilne.	Gosforth.
	Penrith.
	Yorkshire—
Nottinghamshire—	Filey.
Stapleford.	Masham.

The lower part of the shafts of these crosses is cylindrical, and the upper part square. The junction between the two is marked by a band of interlaced work or moulding, above which the square dies off into the round, so that each of the four faces of the upper part terminates at the bottom in a semi-circular end, the convex side pointing downwards. At Penrith, in Cumberland, are a pair of monuments placed 15 ft. apart, with two hog-backed stones between. Perhaps a similar arrangement may have existed in other cases, as at Beckermet St. Bridget's, in Cumberland, there are a pair of pillar crosses, and at Gosforth, in the same county, a second cross formerly existed. Sometimes the shafts are entirely cylindrical and of greater diameter, without any square part, as at Wolverhampton, Masham, and Wilne.

The pillar at Wilne has been converted into a font. The treatment of the decoration of these larger cylindrical crosses is different from that used for the more slender ones, and consists of bands of arcading filled in with figures.

Erect headstones of early date are very rare. The best Saxon example is that of Frithburga at Whitchurch, in Hampshire, already described. Some headstones marked with a plain cross were discovered at Cambridge Castle, together with several slabs covered

with interlaced work, but no headstones with Hiberno-
Saxon ornament upon them have yet been found in
any part of England.

In certain localities a peculiar form of horizontal
body-stone with a coped top was used for placing
over the graves of the Anglo-Saxon Christians.
Monuments of this kind are called hog-backed, from
the shape of the top, which is slightly arched so as
to be higher in the middle than at the two ends.
They are usually about 6 ft. long by 1 ft. 6 in. high,
and the same wide. A ridge runs up the centre of
the stone longitudinally, from which the two sides
slope away like the roof of a house, so that the whole
presents the appearance of a boat turned upside down.
The sloping sides are generally ornamented with scales
to represent the tiling of a roof, and some of the
stones are terminated at each end by beasts facing
each other and grasping the sides with their paws.
The earlier coped stones are hog-backed and decorated with interlaced work, but the later ones have the
top ridge quite horizontal, and arcading round the
sides. It would appear that these coped stones are
of Saxon or Scandinavian origin rather than Celtic,
as they are not met with at all in Ireland or Wales.

The following table shows their geographical distribution :—

Cheshire—
  West Kirkby.
Cornwall—
  Trevillet.
Cumberland—
  Plumbland.
Derbyshire—
  Bakewell.

Derbyshire—
  Darley Dale.
  Repton.

Durham—
  Dinsdale.
  Durham.
  Sockburn.

Kent—
Canterbury.
Fordwich.
Lancashire—
Heysham.
Northamptonshire—
Peterborough.
Northumberland—
Falstone.
Hexham.
Simonburn.
Notts—
Hickling.
Yorkshire—
Bedale.

Yorkshire—
Brompton.
Burnsall.
Dewsbury.
Ingleby Arncliffe.
York.
Kirkby Malzeard.

Scotland—
Abercorn.
Brechin.
Govan.
Inchcolm.
Luss.
Meigle.

At Bexhill, in Sussex, is a small stone covered with interlaced work of rather different shape from any of the above, being in the form of a rectangular truncated pyramid.

Saxon coffin-lids, with a cross running down the centre and the blank spaces on each side filled in with interlaced work, are not uncommon in East Anglia. A large number were found at Cambridge Castle, and others have been dug up at Peterborough[1] and Lincoln Cathedrals, at Rockland, in Norfolk, and Hackthorne, in Lincolnshire. These coffin-lids are probably all of late date, as they approach very nearly to the twelfth and thirteenth-century types of sepulchral slab.

The ornamental features of the Christian monuments of the Anglo-Saxon period in England, like the

[1] The most elaborately ornamented of these slabs was found *in situ* in the north transept in 1888, during the recent restorations in connexion with the fall of the central tower. The erect footstone still remained in a broken condition, but the headstone was gone.

inscriptions, show admixture of the Saxon, the
Scandinavian, and Celtic elements, the predominance
of any one of the three varying according to the
locality. In Northumbria the influence of the Christian art, which was brought over by St. Columba
from Ireland to Iona, and thence was carried by his
disciple, St. Aidan, to Lindisfarne, is apparent in the
designs upon sculptured stones. The ornament on
them is designed with that exquisite finish and com-
pleteness which characterises the best Irish art, and,
with the exception of the graceful scrolls of foliage,
all the patterns correspond with those in the Hiberno-
Saxon MSS. In the Isle of Man and the coast of
Cumberland opposite, certain purely Scandinavian
patterns, composed of chains of rings linked together,
are found upon the crosses, and even stories taken
from Northern mythology, such as those of Sigurd and
Fafner, of the bound Loké, and of Velund the Smith,
are represented on the figure-sculpture, side by side
with the cross of Christ. The interpretation of the
scenes sculptured on the Gosforth Cross by the Rev.
W. S. Calverley, in the "Archæological Journal"
(vol. xl. p. 143), and the Paper on the Leeds Cross,
by the Rev. Prof. G. F. Browne, in the "Journal of
the British Archæological Association" (vol. xli.
p. 131), should be consulted by those wishing to
pursue this line of investigation further. The cross
at Kirk Andreas, in the Isle of Man, with the representations of Sigurd, Fafner, and Loké upon it, is
described in Papers by J. R. Allen, in the "Journal
of the British Archæological Association" (vol. xliii.
p. 260), and by W. G. Black, in the "Proceedings of

the Society of Antiquaries of Scotland" (vol. xxi. p. 325). For cross at Halton, Lancashire, with a blacksmith carved on one of the panels, see "Journ. Brit. Archæol. Assoc.," vol. xlii. p. 328.

The art of the sculptured stones in the South of England is, as a rule, very inferior to that found in the North. The overlapping of the interlaced work is irregular, key-patterns and spirals are entirely absent.

Portable Objects.

Amongst the relics of the Anglo-Saxon Church we shall include not only the vessels and vestments used in religious services, but also any personal ornaments or other objects upon which Christian symbols or figure subjects are represented. The relics of the Anglo-Saxon Church are far less numerous than those of the Irish Church, for in England the shrines of Saints were not carried about for curing diseases, for swearing on, or for obtaining victory in battle[1] to anything like the same extent as was the case in Ireland, and there were no hereditary keepers to hand them down from one generation to another. When Christianity superseded Paganism in England, the practice of depositing grave-goods with the body of the deceased was discontinued, except in the case of ecclesiastics.

The number of Christian objects obtained from the

---

[1] The holy corporax cloth of St. Cuthbert was inclosed in a banner to obtain the victory of Neville's Cross in 1346, but this is an exception. The shrine of St. Cuthbert had a keeper, but his office was not hereditary. (See J. Raine's "St. Cuthbert," pp. 107 and 114.)

Pagan Saxon cemeteries, or from the burial-grounds surrounding early churches, is exceedingly small, and the tombs of the Saxon bishops have nearly all been rifled at the time of the Reformation or some previous period. The body and relics of St. Cuthbert are, perhaps, the only ones which have escaped entire destruction. The account of the adventures by sea and land which these relics have passed through in the course of the 1200 years that have elapsed since St. Cuthbert's death reads more like a Mediæval romance than sober history, and would be wholly incredible had we not the unimpeachable testimony of eye-witnesses as to the truth of the narrative, corroborated by the internal evidence afforded by the objects discovered in the tomb at Durham. The story is begun by the Venerable Bede in his "Ecclesiastical History," where the death and burial of the Saint is described; it is continued by Reginald, a monk of Durham, in the twelfth century, and concluded by the Rev. James Raine, who summarises the whole in his "St. Cuthbert." The facts are briefly these: St. Cuthbert, the sixth bishop of Lindisfarne, died on the Great Farne Island on the 20th of March, A.D. 687. Afterwards "the body of the venerable father was placed on board a ship, and carried to the island of Lindisfarne. It was there met by a large crowd of persons singing psalms, and placed in the Church of the holy Apostle Peter, in a stone coffin on the right side of the altar" (Bede's "Life of St. Cuthbert," ch. xl.). Eleven years later (A.D. 698), the monks of Lindisfarne asked and received permission from Bishop Eadbert to exhume

St. Cuthbert's bones, "intending to put them in a new coffin, and place them, indeed, on the same spot, but above the pavement, on account of the reverence due to him" (Bede's "Eccl. Hist.," bk. iv. ch. xxx.). When the sepulchre was opened the body was found to be entire, presenting the appearance of one asleep rather than dead, and even the vestments still preserved their original freshness. The brethren removed part of the vestments which had enwrapped the body of the saint to take them to Bishop Egbert, who, having received these relics with considerable emotion, ordered the body to be wrapped in a new vestment and placed in a new coffin laid on the pavement of the sanctuary. Bishop Egbert dying soon after "they laid his body in the sepulchre of the blessed Father Cuthbert, placing above it the coffin in which they had deposited the uncorrupted limbs of the same father" (Bede's "Eccl. Hist.," bk. iv. ch. xxx.). For the space of 177 years the remains of St. Cuthbert occupied this position undisturbed, but in A.D. 875, during the bishopric of Eardulf, the monks were obliged to fly from the island to escape the fury of the Danish invaders, taking the coffin which contained the body of St. Cuthbert with them. For eight years (A.D. 875 to 883) the monks wandered from place to place with the relics of the saint, and having remained a short time at Crayke, they at last settled down at Chester-le-Street, in the county of Durham. The story of their wanderings is told by Simeon of Durham,[1] a writer of the eleventh century. He relates that at one time they had even intended to seek

[1] "Surtees Soc. Publications," vol. li., and also Rolls Series.

refuge in Ireland, but after having put to sea were driven back by a storm.   It was during this eventful voyage that the great book of the Lindisfarne Gospels (now in the British Museum) fell into the sea, and was subsequently found by the monks high and dry on the sands at Whithorn, co. Galloway.   St. Cuthbert's body remained at Chester-le-Street for 112 years (A.D. 883 to 995), at the end of which time the bishop and clergy had again to fly before the Danes, on this occasion seeking safety at first at Ripon and shortly after at Durham.   The most important event in connexion with St. Cuthbert's shrine during this period was the visit of King Athelstan in person (A.D. 934–938), who presented numerous costly gifts, including a copy of the Gospels, which perished in the Cottonian fire at the British Museum in 1731.   Its press mark in the Cottonian Library was Otho, B. 9, and an accurate account of it has been preserved by Wanley.   The "Liber Vitæ,"[1] which formerly lay on the high altar at Durham Cathedral and is now in the Chapter Library, contains a list of all the benefactors to St. Cuthbert's Church from the very original foundation thereof, beginning from the ninth century.   The coffin of St. Cuthbert, on being brought to Durham, was first placed in a temporary wooden church, where it remained for three years, until, in A.D. 999, a more worthy stone building was prepared for its reception by Bishop Aldhune.

The body of St. Cuthbert has remained at Durham ever since, except on one occasion when it was taken to Lindisfarne for a year (A.D. 1069–1070) to escape

[1] "Surtees Soc. Publications," vol. xiii.

the threatened vengeance of William the Conqueror. Aldhune's church was pulled down in A.D. 1093, and the present cathedral commenced by Bishop William de St. Carilef; but before one stone of the older building was disturbed, he "prepared a fine, and beautiful tomb of stone in the Cloyster Garth, a yard above the ground, where St. Cuthbert was deposited in expectation of a shrine in the new church, over which was laid a large and beautiful broad marble."

When the new cathedral was ready for the reception of the body, a day was appointed for the solemn removal (Aug. 29, A.D. 1104). It was resolved by the brethren, however, that as no one was alive who could give accurate information about the real contents of the coffin of the saint, it should be opened and examined before its removal to the new cathedral. The brethren therefore appointed for the purpose, nine in number, with Turgot their Prior, having qualified themselves with fasting and prayer, on the 24th of August, as soon as it was dark, prostrated themselves before the venerable coffin, and amid tears and prayers tried to open it with trembling hands.

There are two contemporary accounts of the result of this investigation, one by an anonymous writer and the other by Reginald, a monk of Durham living in the twelfth century. Two separate wooden coffins were opened, one within the other. The outer one is described as "a chest covered on all sides with hides, carefully fixed to it with iron nails," and the inner one as "a coffin of wood, which had been covered all over by coarse linen cloth of a threefold texture, of the length of a man, and covered with a lid of the same description." This was none other than the original coffin made A.D. 698, in which the body had been carried about in its different wanderings. After removing the linen covering, the lid was lifted, and underneath was found a second lid, placed a little lower down, resting on three cross-bars. It was provided with a ring at each end for lifting, and on its upper surface rested a copy of the Gospels. On removing the second lid the body of the saint was disclosed wrapped in three distinct coverings,—(1) a robe of a costly kind, (2) a purple dalmatic, and (3) linen swathings. The body was taken out of the coffin, and, "in addition to the robes which he already wore, they clothed it with the most costly pall which they could find in the church, and over this they placed a covering of the finest linen."

The relics accompanying the body consisted of the bones of Bede and other saints, the head of the blessed King and Martyr Oswald, an ivory comb, a pair of scissors, a silver altar, a linen cloth for covering the sacramental elements, a paten, and a chalice with an onyx stone bowl supported on a gold lion.

The following additional particulars about the inner coffin, in which St. Cuthbert was first placed, in the Island of Lindisfarne (A.D. 698), are given by the monk Reginald, who had seen it himself: "the coffin is made entirely of black oak . . . The whole of it is externally carved with very admirable engraving, of such minute and most delicate work that the beholder, instead of admiring the skill or power of the carver, is lost in amazement. The compartments are very circumscribed and small, and they are occupied by various beasts, flowers, and images, which seem to be inserted, engraved, or furrowed in the wood."

The nave and two side aisles of the cathedral at Durham, begun by Carileph, terminated in three semi-circular apses at the east end, and the relics of St. Cuthbert were placed within a costly shrine or feretory in the middle of the central apse immediately behind the high altar, resting in an elevated position on a stone base, supported by nine pillars of the same material. Lamps were kept perpetually burning round the shrine, maintained by grants made for this special purpose, and the presents left by visitors were suspended all about it. In A.D. 1372 John, Lord Neville of Raby, gave £200 to provide a new base of marble and alabaster for the shrine to rest upon. The work was finished in 1380, in which year the High Altar was solemnly dedicated in honour of St. Mary the Virgin, St. Oswald the Martyr, and St. Cuthbert. The shrine occupied the same position from A.D. 1104, when it was first placed in Carileph's Cathedral until the Dissolution, A.D. 1540 to 1542, but the surroundings were entirely changed by the removal of the apse at the east end of the Norman choir, and the construction of the Chapel of the Nine Altars (A.D. 1233), which is still in existence. In 1540 to 1542 the shrine was destroyed by the orders of King Henry VIII., and the coffin broken open, but after being removed temporarily to the vestry, it was buried under the exact spot which the shrine had formerly occupied, and covered with a "faire marble stone," measuring 8 ft. 11 in. long by 4 ft. 4 in. wide.

On the 17th of May, 1827, the grave of St. Cuthbert was examined in the presence of several of the officers of the cathedral, including the Rev. James Raine, the Librarian, who has given an accurate account of the discoveries then made in his "St. Cuthbert." On removing the marble slab in the pavement and about 18 inches of soil below, a second slab of slightly smaller dimensions was disclosed. This on being lifted was found to cover a grave with side walls of freestone, 7 ft. long by 4 ft. wide and 4 ft. to 5 ft. deep, in which was deposited the coffin of St. Cuthbert. The coffin on being opened was found to enclose a second one, and this again contained a third with the body of the saint in it. All three coffins were of wood; the outer one, that of 1541-1542, was a rectangular coffin made of oak planks 1¾ in. thick, and had three iron rings at each side and one at each end by which it was lowered into the grave; the second was of oak, 1 in. thick, and from its having what appeared to be portions of decayed skin attached to it, was probably the coffin of A.D. 1104; and the third or innermost one was of oak ¾ in. thick and was, as will be seen, the original coffin of A.D. 698, in which the body was placed at Lindisfarne eleven years after St. Cuthbert's death. The innermost coffin corresponds exactly with the description given of it by the anonymous monk and by Reginald, being covered with incised carvings executed with a knife or sharp-pointed instrument. The coffin was removed in fragments, the largest of which did not exceed 2 ft. in length. These fell to still smaller pieces afterwards, but what remain are still carefully preserved in the Cathedral Library at Durham. The carvings represent Apostles, Saints, the Virgin and Child, and the Symbols of the four Evangelists. The names are in each case inscribed in Saxon capitals corresponding with those in the Lindisfarne Gospels, written A.D. 698 to 721, in every instance except one where the abbreviated word "Sanctus" $\overline{SCS}$ occurs in Anglian Runes. The names are as follows :—SS. John, Mark, Thomas, Peter, Andrew, Matthew, Michael, Paul, James, and Luke.

The body of St. Cuthbert was wrapped in a linen winding-sheet, only a few discoloured portions of which remained, and five silken robes: (1) ornamented with gold leaf on an amber ground, the subject being a huntsman with hawk and hound within a cusped medallion, the straight border of the robe having a row of rabbits upon it; (2) ornamented with a ship and pairs of geese swimming on each side together with six fish, the whole surrounded by a circular border of grapes, apples, and pears, outside which are two more geese; (3) ornamented with diaper pattern on an amber ground, and having a lace border; (4) ornamented with crosses—colours purple and crimson; (5) ornamented with oval medallions enclosing an urn supported by griffins on each side; colours crimson and purple.

Most remarkable of all, however, were the stole and maniple with figures and inscriptions embroidered in gold, crimson blue, and green. The stole, which is a narrow band worn round the neck with the two ends hanging down at each side in front, has in the centre of its length a quatrefoil medallion enclosing the Lamb of God, inscribed,—

"AGNV D̄Ī,"

and at the two ends on both back and front square panels, that at one end on the front enclosing a half-length figure of St. John the Evangelist, inscribed,—

"IOHANNES EVC,"

and that on the back containing the following inscription only :—

" ÆLFFLÆD FIERI PRECEPIT "

(Ælfflæd ordered it to be made);
The panel at the other end of the stole, on the front, encloses a half-length figure of St. Thomas the Apostle, inscribed,—

"THOMAS APOST,"

and the panel on the reverse side an inscription only,—

" PIO EPISCOPO FRIDESTANO "
(For the pious Bishop Frithestan).

The intermediate spaces between the panels at the end and the central medallion are occupied by figures of the Prophets Isaiah, Jeremiah, Daniel, Amos, Obadiah, Hosea, Joel, Habaccuc, Jonah, Zechariah, and Nahum, with their names inscribed.

The maniple, which was a narrow band worn over

R

the wrist, is similar in design to the stole.   In the
centre of its length is a quatrefoil medallion, enclosing
the Right Hand of God, the symbol of the First
Person of the Trinity, inscribed,—

"DEXTERA D̄Ī."

At the two ends are square panels on each side of
the stole, that at one end on the front enclosing a half-
length figure of Peter the Deacon, inscribed,—

"PETRVS DIACONVS,"

and that on the back the same inscription as on the
stole,—

"PIO EPISCOPO FRIDESTANO."

The other square termination has on the front a half-
length figure of St. James the Apostle, inscribed,—

"IACOBVS ĀPŌ,"

and on the back the inscription,—

"ÆLFFLÆD FIERI PRECEPIT,"

as on the stole.

The spaces between the central medallion and the
square terminal panels are filled in with figures of
SS. Gregory Pope, John the Baptist, Sixtus Bishop,
and Lawrence Deacon, with their names inscribed.

Frithestan was Bishop of Winchester (A.D. 905 to
932), and Ælfflæd who died in A.D. 916 was queen of
Edward the Elder.   It seems probable that the stole
and maniple found in St. Cuthbert's coffin are the

same which are specified as having been given to his shrine by Athelstan, the illegitimate son of the above-named King Edward, on the occasion of his visit to Chester-le-Street in A.D. 934.

The other relics removed from the coffin of St. Cuthbert in 1827, and deposited in the Cathedral Library at Durham, are,—(1) a "burse" or small linen bag for holding the sacramental elements ; (2) a girdle and two bracelets of gold tissue, probably the gift of Athelstan; (3) a second maniple of the thirteenth century; (4) an ivory comb ; (5) a portable altar of wood plated with silver, inscribed on the back,—

"IN   HONOR(EM)   S.   PETRU ";

and (6) a pectoral cross of gold.

The chalice, paten, and scissors, spoken of by Reginald as having been replaced in the coffin in A.D. 1104, were not found, and probably disappeared when the shrine was destroyed at the time of the dissolution.   St. Cuthbert's ring is now at St. Cuthbert's College, at Ushaw, near Durham ("Archæologia Æliana," N.S., pt. 6, p. 66), and the MS. of St. John's Gospel, removed from the coffin in A.D. 1104, is at Stonyhurst College.   The remains of St. Cuthbert's body were reinterred in the same grave from which they were exhumed in 1827, but the relics were deposited in the Cathedral Library, where they may still be seen.   The Rev. James Raine's " St. Cuthbert " and the publications of the Surtees Society contain all the information that has been collected on the subject.   The reader is also recommended to read Canon Greenwell's address on Durham Cathedral

(Andrews & Co., Durham). Space does not admit of a lengthy description of all the Christian objects of the Anglo - Saxon period, and therefore we must be content to give merely a list of the more interesting specimens with references to the works to be consulted for further details.

Personal Ornaments.—Crosses.

Splendid gold necklace in perfect condition, consisting of 37 beads and pendants with a small cross in centre, found in Anglo-Saxon cemetery at Desborough, Northamptonshire, with a bronze vessel and glass vases; now in the British Museum ("Archæologia," vol. xlv. p. 466).

Gold pendant cross with coin of Heraclius [1] (A.D. 610 to 641) in the centre, and arms ornamented with settings of garnet arranged in geometrical patterns; found in a gravel pit at Lakenheath, near Brandon, in Suffolk, in 1851; now in the British Museum ("Journ. Brit. Archæol. Assoc.," vol. viii. p. 139; and Norfolk Archæol. Journ. for 1860).

Gold pendant cross very similar to the last, except that there is no coin in the centre, found with a circular gold ornament and several pieces of iron at Ixworth, in Suffolk, in 1856; now in the possession of Mr. Joseph Warren (Roach Smith's "Collectanea Antiqua," vol. iv. p. 162).

Gold pendant cross, ornamented with filigree work and a cut garnet in the centre, found in a barrow on

---

[1] A necklace with a circular enamelled pendant and two coins suspended by loops on each side, one being a coin of Heraclius, was found at Sarre, in Kent ("Archæol. Cant.," vol. iii. p. 44).

Winster Moor in 1776 ; now in the Sheffield Museum ("Descriptive Catalogue of the Antiquities in the Museum of T. Bateman, at Lomberdale House, Derbyshire," p. 153).

Silver pendant cross with central boss of variegated glass, found near Gravesend, with Saxon coins (A.D. 814 to 878) ; now in the British Museum ("Numismatic Chronicle," vol. iii. p. 34).

Pair of small pendant silver crosses, found in a woman's grave under tumulus, on Kingston Down, Kent, with a large number of other objects ; now in the Mayer Museum at Liverpool (B. Faussett's "Inventorium Sepulchrale," p. 66, and pl. iv. No. 21).

Small silver cross found in a woman's grave under tumulus on Chartham Down, Kent, with two silver rings and three beads ; now in the Mayer Museum at Liverpool (B. Faussett's "Inventorium Sepulchrale," p. 169, and pl. xi., No. 17).

In the churchyard of St. Martin s, Canterbury, a Saxon necklace was dug up, which it has been endeavoured to associate with Luidhard, the chaplain of Queen Bertha. The necklace, which is now in the Mayer Museum at Liverpool, has attached to it by loops, in the usual way, a Roman intaglio, a circular pendant of gold ornamented with glass, and Merovingian gold coins. One of these is inscribed, "LYUPARDVS EPS," which Dr. D. Haigh twists about in a most ingenious way until he extracts "LVIDHARD" out of it ("Archæol. Cant.," vol. viii. p. 233 ; Roach Smith, "Coll. Ant.," vol. i. p. 176 ; "Numismatic Chron.," vol. vii.).

Personal Ornaments.—Rings.

Gold ring ploughed up between Aberford and Sherburn in Yorkshire; the surface engraved and partly filled in with niello; in the centre of the bezel is the Agnus Dei and the letters "A D"; on the inside of the ring is inscribed the name of Queen Æthelsvith :—

"+ EATHELSVITH REGNA,"

who was the daughter of Ethelwulf, wife of Burgred, King of Mercia, and sister of Alfred the Great (A.D. 854-889); now in the collection of Canon Greenwell ("Proc. Soc. Ant., Lond.," vol. vi., Ser. 2, p. 305).

Ring of Ethelwulf, King of Wessex (A.D. 836-838), and father of Alfred the Great, ornamented with a pair of beasts in enamel, and inscribed,—

"+ ETHELVVLF R,"

found in the parish of Laverstock, Hampshire (Shaw's "Dresses and Decorations of the Middle Ages").

Gold ring of Alhstan, Bishop of Sherborne (A.D. 817-887) found in Caernarvonshire.

Personal Ornaments.—Miscellaneous.

King Alfred's jewel mounted in gold, with a figure holding a flower in each hand on the front and foliageous ornament on the back; inscribed round the edge,—

"+ ALFRED MEC HEHT GEVVRCAN"

(Alfred ordered me to be made),

found in 1693 near Athelney, Somersetshire; now in

the Ashmolean Museum at Oxford (Shaw's "Dresses and Decorations of the Middle Ages").

Situlæ.

Bucket, 6 in. high and 4 in. in diameter, covered with metal plates, having on them in *repoussé* work the Chi-Rho monogram, and the Alpha and Omega within a circle ; the miracle of Cana ; the Baptism of Christ inscribed **IΩANNHC** ; and the Annunciation ; found in a Saxon grave at Long Whittenham, Berkshire ; now in the Mayer Museum at Liverpool ("Archæologia," vol. xxxviii. p. 327).

Cylindrical bronze box or bucket, covered with metal plates, bearing representations in *repoussé* work of a group of three figures six times repeated, the central figure enthroned and nimbed ; over the head of the one on the right a dove holding a crown in its mouth, and over the head of the one on the left a cross, found in a Saxon grave at Strood in 1852 (Roach Smith's "Collectanea Antiqua," vol. ii. p. 158).

Ivories.

Plaque, with Adoration of the Magi (South Kensington Museum, No. 142–66).

Plaque, with Descent from the Cross (South Kensington Museum, No. 3–12).

Plaque, with Christ showing his wounds ; inscribed in Saxon capitals, found at Elmham, Norfolk, now in the Cambridge Antiquarian Museum.

Frank's Casket, with Adoration of the Magi, Flight of the Jews from Jerusalem, &c., and Runic inscriptions, now in the British Museum ("Yorkshire

Archæol. Journ.," vol. ii. p. 256, and Palæographical Soc. Publ.).

Diptych, with Christ treading on the Asp and Basilisk; the Annunciation and Salutation, inscribed in Saxon capitals, taken from the Church of St. Martin, at Genoels Elderen, Limburg, now in Brussels Museum (Westwood's " Miniatures ").

Comb, inscribed in Anglian Runes, with words meaning, " May God bless us, may God Almighty help our kin "; found in the kitchen midden of the ancient monastery at Whitby (" Yorkshire Archæol. Journ.," vol. ii. p. 279).

Seals.

Seal of Godgytha, a nun, and Godwin, a Thane, inscribed in Anglo-Saxon capitals; on the top two enthroned and nimbed figures, perhaps intended for' the Trinity, the dove being broken away; found at Wallingford, Berks; now in the British Museum (" Proc. Soc. Ant., Lond.," vol. viii., Ser. ii. p. 468).

Miscellaneous.

Silver plate with figure of a saint done in *repoussée* work found at Hexham, now in the British Museum (J. Raine's " Priory Church of Hexham," Surtees Soc. Publ., vol. xlvi. p. clxxxii.).

Small leaden coffer with cross and interlaced work, in Lewes Museum.

Leaden book-cover with an Anglo-Saxon inscription from Ælfric's Homilies, in Londesborough Coll. (" Archæologia ").

Anglo-Saxon knife, inscribed in Saxon capitals; in British Museum (" Archæologia," vol. xliv. p. 331).

INDEX.

PRINTED BY THE HANSARD PUBLISHING UNION, LIM.,
GREAT QUEEN STREET, LONDON, W.C.